Boston

A Pictorial Celebration

Jonathan M. Beagle, Ph.D.

Photography by Elan Penn

Sterling Publishing Co., New York
A Sterling Book

Design by Michel Opatowski
Edited by Jacqueline Mulhern
Layout by Gala Pre Press Ltd.

Grateful acknowledgement is made to the following for
use of their photographs:

Boston Public Library, Print Department, 6, 8, 11, 12, 15, 16, 18, 20

New England Aquarium, 111

Library of Congress Cataloging-in-Publication Data is Available

Beagle, Jonathan.
Boston—a pictorial celebration / by Jonathan Beagle ; photography by Elan Penn.
    p. cm.
Includes index.
ISBN-13: 978-1-4027-1977-6
ISBN-10: 1-4027-1977-9
    1. Historic sites—Massachusetts—Boston. 2. Historic
Building—Massachusetts—Boston. 3. Boston (Mass.)—Description and
travel. 4. Boston (Mass.)—Pictorial works. 5. Boston (Mass.)—
Buildings, structures, etc. 6. Boston (Mass.)—History—Miscellanea.
I. Penn, Elan. II. Title.

F73.37.B363 2006
974.4'61—dc22   2005057590

2 4 6 8 10 9 7 5 3 1

Published by Sterling Publishing Co., Inc.
387 Park Avenue South, New York, NY 10016
© 2006 by Penn Publishing Ltd.
Distributed in Canada by Sterling Publishing
c/o Canadian Manda Group, 165 Dufferin Street,
Toronto, Ontario, Canada M6K 3H6
Distributed in the United Kingdom by GMC Distribution Services,
Castle Place, 166 High Street, Lewes, East Sussex,
England BN7 1XU
Distributed in Australia by Capricorn Link (Australia) Pty. Ltd.
P.O. Box 704, Windsor, NSW 2756, Australia

Sterling ISBN-13: 978-4027-1977-6
ISBN-10: 1-4027-1977-9

For information about custom editions, special sales, premium and
corporate purchases, please contact Sterling Special Sales
Department at 800-805-5489 or specialsales@sterlingpub.com.

Opposite: View of Boston across the Charles River.

Contents

Boston: The City Upon a Hill

Its Indian name was Shawmut, but the English would call it Boston. Arriving at the hilly little peninsula in the fall of 1630, the first "Bostonians" did not expect to stay long. Their religious consciences had compelled them, albeit reluctantly, to leave an England that had seemingly strayed from the path of righteousness. Though others may have scoffed at the idea, these so-called Puritans were determined to save their beloved homeland through an inspiring display of Christian living in the American wilderness—a "City upon a Hill," as Governor John Winthrop famously described it. They would return triumphantly once England had seen the error of its ways and reformed. It was an admirably idealistic plan, the failure of which would ironically produce one of the great American cities.

The Puritans, a group of English Protestants who advocated strict religious discipline along with simplification of the ceremonies and creeds of the Church of England, came to Boston perhaps by fate or fortune, but the exact reason is not known.

After enduring storms and sickness on the high seas, the Winthrop fleet reached Cape Ann and the tiny fishing village of Salem in June of 1630. The sudden influx of nearly 1,000 settlers overwhelmed Salem's meager resources, however, and prompted a removal farther down the Massachusetts coastline to Charlestown, Boston's "Mother City" as it would be known. The lure of fresh spring water subsequently carried some, including Governor Winthrop, across the Charles River to Shawmut Peninsula. Connected to the mainland by a thin strip of land that flooded during storms and high tides, the peninsula was a mere two miles long and one mile wide, hardly the sort of place one would expect to find what quickly became the largest city in seventeenth-century America.

The rapid success of Boston surprised even its founders. Clustered around the East Cove, with Beacon Hill at their backs, they carved out a living mostly from the sea. Merchants joined ministers as community leaders, financing the construction of wharves and market houses that soon made Boston the commercial hub of New England. John Josselyn was reminded of London as he walked Boston's cobblestone streets and marveled at its many shops and ships in 1663. Such prosperity seemed a sign of God's favor, although some residents worried that it would also prove the town's undoing. Not only was the seaport attracting some unsavory characters, from rowdy sailors to licentious strumpets, but it also seemed dangerously close to replacing God with Mammon. "[T]ho' they wear in their Faces the Innocence of Doves, you will find them in their Dealings, as Subtile as Serpents," complained one visitor. "Interest is their Faith, Money their God, and Large Possessions the only Heaven they covet."

Faneuil Hall in 1775, 1888 facsimile etching of original engraving from the Massachusetts Magazine of 1789.

A View on Boston Common

Royal officials also cast a suspicious eye upon Bostonians, whom they long considered disloyal for leaving England and criticizing both the Crown and its Anglican Church. In the 1680s, they took the bold step of stripping the Massachusetts Bay Colony of its self-governing charter and installed a new regime headed by an English aristocrat. Boston would never be quite the same again. Its inhabitants learned to jealously guard their liberty, for although England's Glorious Revolution of 1688 would win them back many former privileges, they lost the right to elect their own governor. They were also forced to tolerate non-Puritans in their community. For some, it felt like the end of the world. To others, it was a new beginning.

The political, economic, and religious changes that transformed Boston in the eighteenth century were also reflected in its evolving architecture. Plain, wooden meetinghouses gave way

Cows grazing on Boston Common under a single large tree with the Back Bay in the distance and Beacon Street to the right, circa 1815.

gardens bespoke the wealth of the merchant class, a two-story workhouse told a different story about growing problems with poverty and unemployment. The population even temporarily ebbed from its high water mark of around 16,000 in the 1740s, as high taxes, price inflation, and currency shortages drove some inhabitants to seek greener pastures elsewhere.

By the time of the American Revolution, Boston was no longer the largest or most urbane of Britain's colonial cities, an honor that belonged to Philadelphia. Yet it was more identifiably English than arguably any other part of His Majesty's North American Empire. "This is more like an English Old Town than any in America," noted Lord Adam Gordon, "the Language and manner of the people very much resemble the old Country." As such, Bostonians believed they shared the same political rights as those living in London itself. When Parliament suggested otherwise, they launched a revolution to protect ancient liberties handed down from their Puritan ancestors.

Even after the colonists broke from Britain and assumed a new identity as Americans, Bostonians remained deeply attached to their English roots. Some simply refused to leave the Empire and in 1776 fled to Canada, where many of their ancestors remain today. Those who remained were later reluctant to go to war against Britain again in 1812, and a few even suggested New England's secession from the United States as a possible alternative. Visiting Boston in 1837, the Englishman Francis Marryat was pleased to learn that the inhabitants "consider themselves, and pride themselves, as

to brick and stone churches capped with towering steeples, the skyscrapers of their day. Puritan Congregational churches still dominated the religious landscape, but Anglican (Church of England), Quaker, Baptist, and Huguenot houses of worship were now visible as well. The monarch's authority over the community was evident in the royal emblems that covered the State House on recently renamed King Street. And while fine Georgian mansions and English being peculiarly English, while, on the contrary, the majority of Americans deny that they are English." Twenty years later another observer similarly concluded, "A Bostonian . . . is still an Englishman in America."

Although England was historically the barometer by which Bostonians measured their civility, they also saw themselves competing with rival American cities for cultural authority over the new nation. They staked their claim through urban improvements, education, and cultivation of the arts, all of which were funded with new sources of wealth. Boston merchants were among the first to open up the lucrative China trade and to invest in domestic manufacturing after the Revolution. Their civic pride was evident not only in the institutions they founded, but also in the nicknames Bostonians gave their city: "The Athens of America," "The Venice of America," and "The Hub of the Universe."

Beacon Hill

No section of the city better reflects the value of Proper Boston than Beacon Hill. As the address of the Massachusetts State House, its name has become synonymous with wealth and power, but it originally referred to a wooden beacon placed there to alert the community of danger. The largest prominence on Shawmut Peninsula, Beacon Hill was also part of a ridge known as the "Trimountain," from which nearby Tremont Street derives its name. The area experienced little development beyond John Hancock's mansion until after the Revolution, when its south face was chosen as the site for the new State House. Although the building signified Massachusetts's political independence from Britain, its design also reflected Boston's English cultural inheritance. Such a building, concluded one foreign observer, "could have entered into the head of none but an English architect to conceive." In actuality, the architect was a native Bostonian, Charles Bulfinch, who was deter-

mined to refashion Boston in the mold of a great European city.

Bulfinch's State House transformed Beacon Hill into a stylish neighborhood and placed him in great demand among the local elite. He would build many of the beautiful brick homes that still line its streets. Over the years, some of the city's most famous residents have called Beacon Hill home, especially its politicians. In November of 2004, for instance, Democratic presidential candidate John Kerry anxiously awaited election results at his townhouse in Louisburg Square, only to learn of his narrow defeat at the hands of incumbent George W. Bush. Even Charles Bulfinch himself had a home on the Hill.

Bulfinch also designed the original Massachusetts General Hospital, one of several prestigious institutions to gravitate toward Beacon Hill in the early nineteenth century. The Boston Athenaeum was another. It had once been located next to King's Chapel before moving in 1849 to its current location at 10½ Beacon Street. With one of the largest book collections in the country, the Athenaeum helped establish Boston's reputation as the literary capital of the United States and was patronized by such celebrated authors as Nathaniel Hawthorne and Louisa May Alcott.

Just a stone's throw away from the Athenaeum, in Old Granary Burying Ground, lies the grave of Crispus Attucks, victim of the Boston Massacre and the first black martyr to the cause of American liberty. His tragic death became an inspiration to generations of African Americans, including members of the all-black 54th Massachusetts Infantry Regiment, who marched off to glory during the Civil War. Massachusetts may have abolished slavery after the Revolution, but racism was still very much alive in Boston. Blacks had difficulty procuring anything but the most menial of work and were

Hancock House, Beacon Street, 1860.

often segregated in schools and churches, resulting in what some described as an "aristocracy of skin." Many African-American families huddled in tenements on the north slope of Beacon Hill, seemingly a world away from the wealth and splendor of Bulfinch's Boston. At the

African Meeting House on Joy Street, however, they could sing, dance, worship, and learn together without being harassed. The building became the cornerstone of Boston's black community in the nineteenth century and remains a cultural institution today.

displayed in the Back Bay district. The Commonwealth Avenue Mall, patterned after Parisian boulevards of the period, features a tree-lined promenade, grassy expanses, and wide streets with elegant brownstones set back from the roadway. Mansard roofs on many of the homes add to the cosmopolitan character of the neighborhood, though modern traffic congestion does ruin its romantic air a bit. Those seeking an amorous retreat often head instead to the Public Garden, where paddleboats and fragrant flowers are sure to stir the passions. Some visitors even see stars in their eyes, not of the celestial kind but rather the Hollywood type. Actors Grace Kelly, Shirley Temple, Bette Davis, Ted Danson, and director Rob Reiner are among the many celebrities to have enjoyed the Garden's famed Swan Boats.

The fresh flowery scent of the Public Garden replaced the foul stench that had formerly characterized the Back Bay, a muddy tidal basin that doubled as a garbage disposal. A westerly breeze on a warm afternoon often sent people scurrying off Boston Common to avoid the odor. Everyone agreed after the Revolution that the bay should be filled, but for what purpose? Some saw the economic utility of the new land for a growing populace and pushed for residential development. Others, reacting against the noise and congestion of the city, argued for the creation of a new public space to complement the Common.

In the 1850s, with the city's population over 160,000, both visions were implemented as Boston embarked on one of the most ambitious urban development plans of its day, to fill Back Bay with dirt and gravel hauled in by rail from

Back Bay

Paris replaced London as the model for Boston's urban development in the mid-nineteenth century. Though evident elsewhere in the city, the French connection is most dramatically

Needham, Massachusetts. (A similar, though smaller, project had already leveled much of the Trimountain earlier in the century to provide new land for various West End and Beacon Hill neighborhoods.) The massive undertaking created some 400 acres and took decades to complete, but resulted in a fashionable new residential district for the city's upper classes and cultural elite, the so-called Boston Brahmins.

The Gibson House museum on Beacon Street chronicles the Brahmin experience through the eyes of the colorful Charles Gibson, a long-time Back Bay resident. While Gibson wanted to share his privileged lifestyle with the public, members of the exclusive St. Botolph Club prefer to keep theirs private. Described by some as a "last bastion" of elitism, the century-old club once met on Newbury Street, known more recently for its pricey boutiques and cozy restaurants. Early members included the architect H.H. Richardson and The Reverend Phillips Brooks, who together were responsible for one of Boston's architectural marvels, Trinity Church.

Together with Old South Church and the Boston Public Library, Trinity Church illustrates the tendency of many institutions to follow the population into the Back Bay during the 1870s and 1880s. The move allowed them to escape the confines of the old city and expand their roles within the community. With over six million volumes in its possession, the Boston Public Library now ranks among the largest lending libraries in the country, and its collection of rare books and documents draws scholars from all over the world. Trinity Church, located across from the library on scenic Copley Square, has become renowned for more than its world-class choir; it also provides valuable assistance to the disadvantaged and the ill.

The North End and Charlestown

Back Bay's gain was, in certain respects, the North End's loss. As the deepest part of Boston Harbor, the North End had developed a distinctly maritime character in the colonial era. Its busy shipyards employed a wide variety of local craftsmen and laborers who lived in the area, including blacks from the "New Guinea" neighborhood near Copp's Hill. The famed U.S.S. *Constitution*, now on display at the Charlestown Navy Yard, was one of many vessels constructed in Boston's North End. Sailors were also a common sight on its narrow, crowded streets, which were lined with slop-shops and taverns catering to jack tars. The notoriously rough-and-tumble character of the neighborhood gave some pious Puritans pause. The Reverend Cotton Mather, who lived and ministered in the North End, went so far as to make trips down to its dockyards, distributing religious readings amongst the sailors in the hope that they might become good Christians. Whether or not they found God, many mariners did find a final resting place alongside Mather at Copp's Hill Burial Ground.

Despite the North End's rather sordid reputation, a number of wealthy merchants made it their home in order to be near their wharves and warehouses. An early example survives in the form of the Paul Revere House, originally built for the merchant Robert Howard in the 1680s. By the eighteenth century, their luxurious Georgian mansions lent the North End a respectable air, as did the growing numbers of churches their money helped construct. Such riches were occasionally ill gotten, however. Boston was an infamous haven for smugglers and pirates, and some locals were willing to look the other way in dealing with them. Decorative angels on display at Christ Church, now known as Old North, were taken from a French ship bound for Canada and donated by Captain Thomas Gruchy in 1746.

The Revolutionary War hit Boston's North End especially hard. The British occupation and blockade of Boston Harbor severely disrupted commercial trade, putting sailors and mechanics out of work. In turn, the American siege of the

Boston Palace Car, Open car for sightseeing in Boston. Passengers sit on bench seats while the driver and guide, with bullhorn, sit in the front. Sign on car indicates that the car "starts opposite Hotel Touraine at 10-2-4", circa 1910.

seaport prompted undersupplied British soldiers to tear down Cotton Mather's old church and other structures for firewood. Several affluent North End merchants fled Boston with the King's troops in the spring of 1776, taking much of their wealth with them. Afterwards, a smallpox epidemic ravaged the town and spread rapidly through the compact quarters of the North End. "I can't describe the alteration and the gloomy appearance of this Town," James Warren told John Adams. "No Business, no Busy Faces but those of the Physicians. Ruins of buildings, wharfs, etc. etc., wherever you go, and the streets covered with grass."

Boston recovered from the Revolution, and before long the North End wharves were bustling with maritime traffic again. One observer likened the scene to a forest of ship masts floating in the

harbor. But the residential development of Beacon Hill and later Back Bay drew wealthy families away from the North End, which grew increasingly working-class and commercial in character. The arrival of packet lines and the advent of the Irish potato famine brought thousands of poor Irish Catholic immigrants to the North End in the 1840s and 1850s, largely turning it into a tenement district. Some 50,000 Irish inhabited Boston by 1855.

There were definite patterns of settlement among the North End Irish, with immigrants from Cork County concentrating around North Square near the Revere House while those from Donegal gravitated toward the area around Endicott Street. "Cork Hill" and "Galway City" were the nicknames given to different parts of the rapidly changing North End. The Irish moved in as native Bostonians moved out, taking over the buildings they left behind. Hence did the Bulfinch-designed New North Unitarian Church become St. Stephen's Roman Catholic Church in the 1860s.

Toward the end of the nineteenth century, the North End underwent another transformation as Italian immigrants began to displace the Irish. Cultural differences and competition for work canceled out any religious affinity between the two Catholic groups, resulting in significant tension. They generally lived separate lives, with the Italians worshipping at their own churches such as Sacred Heart, but their paths inevitably crossed on the narrow North End streets. "The Irish had gangs on the street corners," recalled one Italian immigrant. "They would stop you and ask for a drink. If you give them a drink, you don't have no beer left, and maybe you get beaten up anyway. If you don't let them have a drink, they take it away from you, drink all the

Feeding the swans in the Public Garden, by Leslie Jones, circa 1920.

beer, and throw the empty can at you." Needless to say, the North End was not a place Boston police enjoyed patrolling in the nineteenth century.

Native Bostonians were initially no more enamored with Italian immigrants than they had been with the Irish decades earlier. "The atmosphere is actually thick with the vile odors of garlic and onions- of macaroni and lazzaroni," they complained. Rather than drive people out, however, such smells have instead attracted them to a gentrified North End in recent years. The neighborhood's Italian restaurants offer some of the best cuisine in Boston, and a North Ender, Guiseppe Parziale, is even credited with introducing pizza to Americans.

The Financial District

Behind the gentrification of Boston's North End lies the revival of its Financial District. Located along State Street, the Financial District has served as the heart of Boston's business community for generations. The Puritan founders first established an open-air provisions market at the site of the Old State House in the 1630s, after which a number of artisans set up their shops in the area. A controversial proposal to move the adjacent town meetinghouse away from the marketplace met with furious resistance from shopkeepers and craftsmen who feared their businesses would suffer. The debate grew so heated that Puritan leaders worried it might tear the community apart in 1639. In the end, the meetinghouse was simply relocated to the opposite side of the market, and trade continued unabated.

The construction of the first Town House atop the marketplace in the 1650s transformed it into a fashionable place for gentleman-merchants to

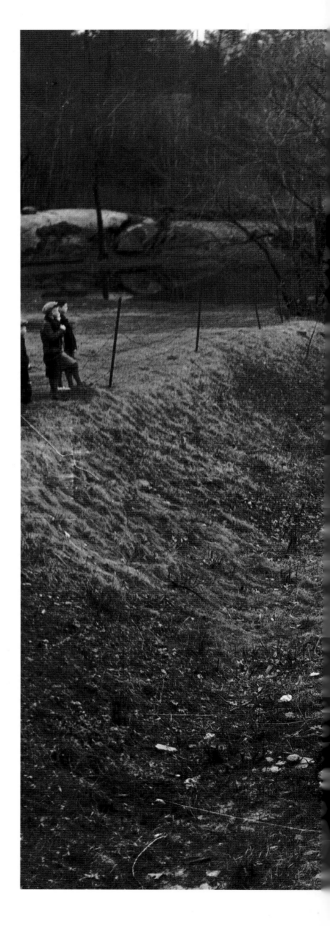

Start of Marathon, by Leslie Jones, 1939.

Group of children pose in front of the Paul Revere House, by Leslie Jones, circa 1954.

meet and discuss business. According to Joseph Bennett, who visited Boston in 1740, "they meet every day at one o'clock, in imitation of the Exchange at London, which they call by the name of Royal Exchange too." Country traders were consequently forced out into the streets to hawk their provisions door-to-door, leaving Boston without a marketplace. While some preferred this system, others complained that it clogged the streets, contributed to growing crime in the community, and generally gave Boston a bad reputation. Theirs was the only city in the British Empire not to possess a market house, a source of embarrassment to proud Bostonians.

When Peter Faneuil remedied the situation

in 1740 by personally financing an elegant brick market named in his honor, he was treated like a hero. Admirers declared Faneuil Hall "a noble building" and praised its patron as "the most public-spirited man . . . that ever yet appeared on the Northern Continent of *America*." Over eighty years later, Mayor Josiah Quincy also gained everlasting fame for expanding and modernizing the marketplace. Along with Ammi Young's 1838 customhouse, the Greek-Revival-style Quincy Market represented the economic vitality and democratic optimism of antebellum Boston. The Financial District flourished, and banks and insurance companies were incorporated at an unprecedented rate.

Yet some became disillusioned by what they saw as the corruptive influence of State Street business values on American democracy and civilization. "The lesson of these days is the vulgarity of wealth," grumbled Ralph Waldo Emerson. "We know that wealth will vote for the same thing which the worst and meanest of the people vote for." The Panic of 1857 and onset of the Civil War in 1861 further shook the city's confidence in its capitalist leaders, as investigations uncovered greed and graft that jeopardized the war effort. Historian Howard Mumford Jones tells the story of indignant soldiers dumping inferior overcoats onto State Street as they marched by. A disappointed Charles Francis Adams believed that conservative Boston businessmen had surrendered the enterprising initiative to rival New York.

As if to prove Adams's point, the design of Boston's Custom House Tower, built in 1915, was curiously imitative of the Metropolitan Life Insurance Building in New York. The landmark tower nonetheless became a symbol of the Financial District's prosperous new heights and stood for decades as Boston's tallest structure. That it now houses luxury time-share suites says as much about the changing nature of Boston's waterfront as it does the renewed affluence of the Financial District.

The Waterfront

It was rather hard to escape the waterfront in Boston's early days. With its lone land entrance prone to flooding, Shawmut Peninsula was nearly an island, and most people traveled to and from the seaport by ship. But it was no easy trip. Boston Harbor had only a single, narrow shipping channel with plenty of rocks and shoals to ensnare the unwary sailor. Captains relied on landmarks such as the Boston lighthouse and Fort William on Castle Island to guide them safely into the town, which cut an impressive figure against the ocean tide. As Abbé Robin's vessel sailed past the islands that dotted the harbor, he spied "a magnificent prospect of houses, built on a curved line, and extending afterwards in a semicircle above half a league. . . . This was Boston," he wrote excitedly in his 1781 journal. "These edifices, which were lofty and regular, with spires and cupolas intermixt at proper distances, did not seem to us a modern settlement so much as an ancient city, enjoying all the embellishments and population, that never fail to attend on commerce and the arts."

The largest ships headed toward Long Wharf, which stretched nearly 2,000 feet into the harbor to welcome them. It was a major engineering feat for eighteenth-century New England and invariably impressed visitors. Many of the smaller wharves and warehouses bore the names of the prominent merchants who built them. Very few still survive from the colonial era. Those that do, such as Rowes Wharf and the Gardner warehouse, exist in much-altered form and function. Long Wharf has been reduced to a shadow of its former self. And gone completely is the Town Dock, replaced by Quincy Market, where oystermen once moored their boats and called out to the locals, "Oise, buy-ni'-oise: here's oise."

Historically, the health of Boston's economy could be gauged by the amount of activity along its waterfront. Trade came to a virtual standstill after the British imposed a naval blockade to punish the seaport for the Boston Tea Party of

1773. The return of peace brought a burst of activity as war-torn inhabitants eagerly consumed goods they had been forced to do without, even those made in England. In fact, their spending spree alarmed some who found it contrary to the spirit of virtuous frugality that had characterized the Revolution. Freed from the restraints of the British Empire, Boston merchants began tapping new international markets, a development reflected in the construction of new piers such as India Wharf in 1803. Maritime traffic grew so heavy in the decades before the Civil War that ships often dropped anchor in the harbor and waited hours for a berth to become available.

Boston's waterfront changed significantly in the twentieth century, however. Whereas the city had once been the main attraction for residents and tourists alike, growing numbers were escaping its confines to frolic along the beaches of Cape Cod and Nantasket. Passenger ferries and pleasure crafts consequently replaced many of the cargo ships that had once dominated the docks. Through such programs as Community Boating, Bostonians discovered the recreational qualities of their waterfront, and marinas at Long Wharf and elsewhere were built to accommodate everything from canoes and sailboats to private yachts. Rowes Wharf was remade into a luxury hotel and office complex, while an old warehouse became the new home of the acclaimed Chart House restaurant. The New England Aquarium and the Boston Children's Museum, the sorts of cultural institutions that in the past would have been located along the Back Bay, instead chose scenic waterfront locations that have further revitalized the district in recent years.

The Fenway

Suburbanization shifted Boston's population away from the once-bustling waterfront toward newly annexed inland areas such as Brighton and West Roxbury by the early twentieth century.

Along with the town of Brookline, which resisted annexation, these westerly districts had been historically agricultural. The swampy salt meadows, or fens, that lined the Charles River and tributaries such as Stony Brook and Muddy River provided hay for livestock, many of which would be driven to the Boston market. In fact, the streets of the seaport became so clogged with swine and other farm animals in the eighteenth century that local officials enacted bylaws to control their numbers.

Trolleys and trains transformed these sleepy rural villages into fashionable neighborhoods for wealthy and cultured Bostonians after the Civil War. Among those who preferred the more intimate setting of Brookline over Boston's immensity was Augustus Lowell and his wife Katherine, whose daughter Amy became a Pulitzer-prize-winning poet and son Percival founded Arizona's Lowell Observatory. Newlyweds Joseph and Rose Kennedy also settled there in 1914, where they raised a future American president as well as a pair of United States Senators. While John F. Kennedy's birthplace is now a National Historic Site, the Brookline home where architect H.H. Richardson died in 1886 has languished to the point where it has become one of Massachusetts's ten most endangered historic resources. "The poor thing is a money pit," admits one preservation official.

Frederick Law Olmsted's idyllic Fairsted estate avoided a similar fate in 1979 when it was named a National Historic Site. As America's premier landscape architect, Olmsted transformed the marshy fens into a shimmering "Emerald Necklace" of public parks in the late nineteenth century. Before the days of movies and television, only Red Sox baseball games at nearby Fenway Park, built in 1912, proved more entertaining for ordinary Bostonians than a daytrip to Olmsted's parks.

The Fenway district became the early twentieth century equivalent of the Back Bay neighborhood fifty years earlier, a presumably tranquil place where the daily commotion of city life could not disturb the artist's eye, the musician's ear, or the teacher's voice. Henry Lee Higginson considered it the perfect location for Symphony Hall, which was soon followed by the Boston Opera House and the New England Conservatory of Music that staffed both institutions. Before building her own "Fenway Court" art museum in 1903, Isabella Stewart Gardner had contemplated donating her sizable collection to the Museum of Fine Arts, which ironically relocated from Copley Square to the Fens just a few years later.

Educational institutions also flourished in the Fenway, including Simmons women's college, the Berklee College of Music, Northeastern University, and the historic Boston Latin School—the oldest public school in America. The Massachusetts Historical Society pioneered this westward intellectual migration when it moved to Boylston Street in 1899. And Boston University finally found a home in the Fenway after spending decades sprawled all over the city, a consolidation commemorated with Marsh Chapel as the new campus center. A few organizations eventually swam against the tide, drawn away from the Fenway by downtown Boston's urban renewal efforts in the post-World War II era, though some, such as the Larz Anderson Auto Museum, found the waters rather choppy and soon returned.

Around the Hub

"As London is to England for priority, so is Boston to this Province," explained Reverend Benjamin Colman to a friend in 1719. While there was much truth to the minister's observation, it also led him to rather arrogantly dismiss other parts of Massachusetts as "a kind of Highlands with us for Incivility and Irreligion, Licentiousness and Ignorance." Colman was not alone in such sentiments. Visitors to the countryside often mocked the efforts of rural families to be as urbane as the Bostonians. It would seem that the city's sense of its self-importance began long before the nineteenth-century notion of Boston as "the hub of the solar system."

Yet Boston's star has never shone so brightly as to obscure its satellites, which sparkle with their own light. As early as 1636, Harvard University marked Cambridge, Massachusetts as an educational center that has even drawn Boston into its orbit. The Weeks Memorial Bridge enables students to shuttle between areas of the campus, which now spans both sides of the Charles River. Harvard has also exerted a gravitational pull on such schools as the Massachusetts Institute of Technology, founded in Boston but moved to Cambridge in 1916.

When the tides of war and revolution briefly eclipsed Boston's radiance in the 1770s and 1780s, other towns blazed new paths. Salem and other Essex County seaports experienced a golden age of commerce as vessels such as the *Friendship* boldly sailed where few New Englanders had gone before, Asia. And as the sun began to set on Britain's American empire at Concord's North Bridge on April 19, 1775, a new dawn emerged there as well. "From the plains of Concord will henceforth be dated a change in human affairs, an alteration in the balance of human power, and a new direction to the course of human improvement," predicted Timothy Dwight in 1796. Like the golden dome of Boston's State House, Massachusetts' brilliant past continues to shine like a beacon, lighting the way toward a brighter future.

Beacon Hill

Massachusetts State House

Although it represents the entire Commonwealth, the golden-domed Massachusetts State House has been one of Boston's most recognizable landmarks for centuries. Independence from Great Britain had rendered the Old State House on State Street obsolete, prompting a movement in the 1780s to build a larger, more fitting structure somewhere else. But where? Some argued that Boston itself was too reminiscent of the old colonial order to act as the new state capital and suggested that a state house be constructed in another town, perhaps Worcester, where a number of Bostonians had fled during the British occupation. The town of Plymouth, which predated Boston by some ten years, also expressed serious interest in becoming the state capital.

Realizing that it was in danger of losing its traditional pre-eminence, Boston bought a plot of land once owned by John Hancock and offered it to the Commonwealth in 1795 as a site for the new state house. The 1.7 acre–Beacon Hill location, which overlooked Boston Common, had several advantages, not the least of which was aesthetic. It was also a relatively undeveloped section of the city that provided plenty of space to build and avoided the crowded conditions that had dogged the Old State House downtown. Officials agreed that it would be an ideal place for a capitol building.

The choice of an architect to design the new state house was simple. Boston native Charles Bulfinch had already made a reputation for himself as a professional architect after building the Hartford State House in Connecticut and the beautiful Boston Theater locally. He was eager to make his hometown the architectural equal of Europe's greatest cities, which he had visited during an extensive tour in 1785 and 1786. According to historian Harold Kirker, Bulfinch's design for the Massachusetts State House was a modified version of the Somerset House of government in London.

Governor Samuel Adams and Paul Revere laid the building's cornerstone on July 4, 1795 in an elaborate ceremony featuring fifteen white horses, one for every state in the Union at the time. During work on the building in 1855, this famed cornerstone and its encapsulated contents underneath, which included early Massachusetts coins and an inscribed silver plate, were found to be in rough shape. They were refurbished and reinserted under a new cornerstone.

Twice during the antebellum era, first in 1831 and then as part of the 1855 construction, new additions were made to the north side of the State House, away from the Common. The interior of the original building was remodeled after the Civil War, and the so-called "Brigham extension" was added to the northern part of the property in the 1890s. These additions and alterations were necessary to keep pace with the state's expanding government and to ensure that the building could continue to function as the capitol. None were allowed to overshadow the architectural elegance of the original structure. The East and West wings of the State House, added between 1914 and 1917, provide a good example, as their simple marble and granite facades stand subordinate to Bulfinch's rich, redbrick design.

The State House's distinctive red bricks were not always so admired, however. They were painted yellow for much of the nineteenth century and only returned to their natural color in 1928. The celebrated golden dome has also undergone several facelifts over the years. In fact, the original Bulfinch dome was made of wood that quickly deteriorated and was sheathed in protective copper provided by Paul Revere's mill in 1802. The dome first became gilded during America's Gilded Age, when twenty-three carat

Previous page: Beacon Hill viewed across the Charles River.

gold leaf was added in 1874. But fear of German air raids during World War II forced the Commonwealth to paint it an unflattering battleship gray for a time. Restoration of its preferred golden hue has become increasingly expensive over the years. The last such project in 1997 cost taxpayers a whopping $300,000.

The Massachusetts State House is not just for public officials to enjoy. Indeed, it has long been a popular tourist attraction. Nineteenth-century travelers to Boston invariably visited the building, and many dared climb to the top of the dome for a spectacular view of the city. The grounds are ornamented with statues of influential Massachusetts citizens such as Civil War general Joseph Hooker and President John F. Kennedy. Sculptures of Anne Hutchinson and Mary Dyer, both of whom were persecuted by Puritan authorities, remind passersby of the importance of religious liberty.

The interior of the State House has become as much a museum as working office space over the years. Memorial Hall, more commonly called the Hall of Flags, once displayed original flags carried by Massachusetts troops into battle, but the stress placed on them prompted their removal in favor of remarkably realistic transparencies in 1987. Included in the collection are hundreds of Civil War flags, but also many flown during the Spanish-American War and each of the major wars of the twentieth century.

The legendary Sacred Cod, which honors the fish's economic importance to the Commonwealth, is a rather unusual specimen that hangs within the House of Representatives' chamber. Originally attached to the Old State House, the wooden cod was removed in 1798 and taken to Bulfinch's newly completed building at the suggestion of merchant John Rowe. It has since become a Massachusetts icon and a prized catch for pranksters.

Robert Gould Shaw / 54th Regiment Memorial

Among the most storied monuments in Boston, the Shaw/54th Regiment memorial honors the courage and sacrifice of the first black volunteer regiment recruited in the North during the Civil War. Enlistees included two sons of the famed abolitionist Frederick Douglass, for whom the regiment represented an opportunity to showcase the skills of black soldiers and destroy Southern slavery in "[o]ne gallant rush." The white officer chosen to command the celebrated regiment was Colonel Robert Gould Shaw, a relatively undistinguished soldier from a distinguished Boston family. Shaw was no abolitionist and worried about the capacity of his men for battle, yet he understood the political importance of the 54th Regiment to both the abolitionist cause and the state of Massachusetts. This significance was reinforced on May 28, 1863, when the city of Boston gave the regiment a grand send-off as it prepared for deployment in South Carolina. The memorial's location across from the State House on Beacon Street marks the parade route taken by the regiment that day. Just two months later, Shaw and over 250 of his soldiers would lose their lives in a failed attempt to capture Fort Wagner, one of several Confederate strongholds guarding the entrance to Charleston Harbor.

Although many members of the 54th regiment performed bravely against superior numbers at Fort Wagner, it was Shaw who garnered most of the attention back in Boston after news of his death reached the city. A committee was created to consider erecting a memorial to the fallen colonel, but the project languished until the 1880s. Finally, twenty years after Shaw's death, the committee selected Augustus Saint-Gaudens, an Irish-born sculptor from New Hampshire, to build the memorial, which went through several incarnations before its official dedication in 1897. When the monument was unveiled to the public, only the names of the regiment's white officers appeared on the granite and marble surrounding the bronze sculpture.

Soldiers and Sailors Monument

Boston has no shortage of memorials honoring the military service of its citizens, yet few match the grandeur of the Soldiers and Sailors Monument. Perched atop Flagstaff Hill, the Civil War-era monument features a 72-foot column with the statue "Genius of America" overlooking Boston Common, an appropriate site given its importance to the city's military traditions. When news of the Confederate attack on Fort Sumter reached Boston in April of 1861, state militia regiments were immediately ordered to muster on the Common, which had served such a function since the seventeenth century. The Common served as a parade ground for various regiments throughout the war, including the famed 54th Massachusetts, while the community used it to celebrate signal Union victories, such as the fall of Richmond on April 3, 1865. Later that same month, Bostonians gathered together on the Common to mourn the death of President Abraham Lincoln.

After the guns fell silent and the scars of war started to heal, local leaders began planning a memorial to recognize victims of the conflict. Instrumental in this process were members of the so-called Union Club, which had been formed in

1863 to support Abraham Lincoln's war aims. From its headquarters on Park Street across from the Common, the Club gathered public support and helped plan its official dedication, held on September 17, 1877 to mark the anniversary of the founding of Boston.

Since its dedication, the Soldiers and Sailors Monument has been included in many of the city's military celebrations and has acquired meaning for veterans of modern wars as well.

Another important monument pays tribute to the founders of the city (below) who arrived after a long sea voyage to the Shawmut Peninsula, as it was known by the Native Americans. The Puritans renamed it Boston shortly after establishing their religious colony in 1630.

Monument commemorating founding of Boston

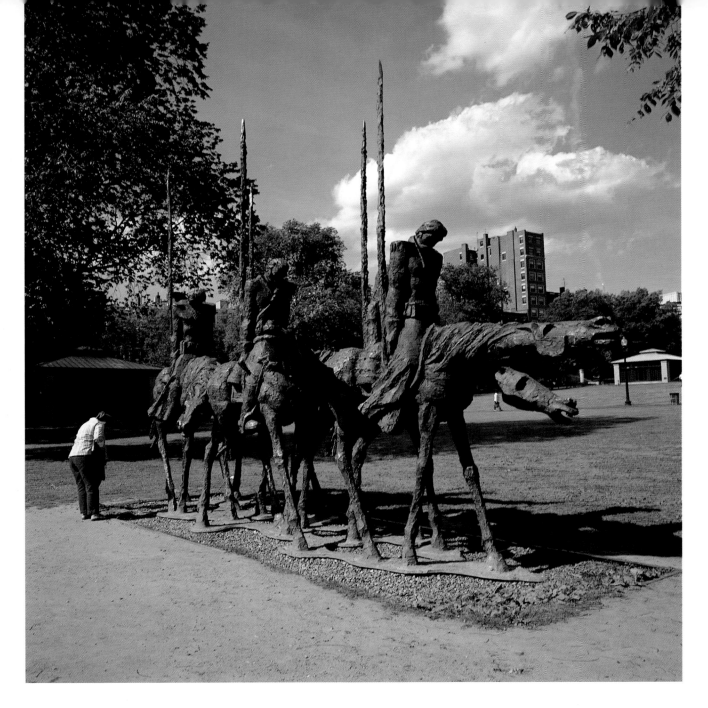

Partisans Statue

There has been no shortage of debate about Andrzej Pitynski's statue *Partisans* since its debut on Boston Common in the early 1980s. Designed as a memorial to those who suffer in the cause of liberty and human rights, the aluminum-cast sculpture depicts five weary Polish freedom fighters on horseback. Pitynski, whose own family had struggled against communism in his native Poland, believed Boston was the best place to display his work because of its historic reputation as the "Cradle of Liberty." The sculpture was originally accepted with the understanding that it was to be a temporary exhibit, which has since become permanent. Situated on Charles Street across from the Public Garden, the sizable statue commands the attention of passersby. Some find it moving; others consider it an eyesore and cannot understand its connection to a city not especially known for its Polish heritage. And although its meaning is universal, the sculpture has arguably lost some of its immediacy in the post-Cold War era. Critics use it as an example of Boston's often-indiscriminate display of public art, along with such curious pieces as the Leif Ericsson statue standing on the Commonwealth Avenue Mall.

King's Chapel

Looking upon King's Chapel today, with its solid granite design, the casual observer would hardly believe that Boston's first Anglican church held a very precarious position in the community after its establishment in 1686. But if one recalls that the city's Puritan founders had left England in 1630 partly to escape persecution from the Church of England, its controversial origins become clearer. Decades of mistrust between the Stuart monarchs and the Massachusetts Puritans led the King to revoke the colony's original charter

of self-governance in 1684 and personally appoint a governor, Sir Edmund Andros, to rule in his name. Already upset by the political changes, Bostonians were further dismayed to learn that Andros was an Anglican who insisted that Church of England religious services be offered in the town, something that had been previously banned.

The building's location on the corner of Tremont and School Street was considered sacred space for the Puritans since it served as their oldest burying ground, which contained the remains of none other than John Winthrop, the colony's first governor.

King's Chapel underwent expansion between 1749 and 1754, employing the designs of Newport, Rhode Island architect Peter Harrison. Much of the King's Chapel interior remains as it appeared in the eighteenth century, including the wooden pulpit hand-crafted by a French Huguenot immigrant. During the Revolutionary War, British officers worshipped at the church and spared it the destruction they visited upon several Congregational churches in town. In fact, following the British evacuation of Boston in 1776, the building was shared with members of the Old South Meetinghouse until repairs to their church were completed. Since it was politically incorrect after Independence to refer to the structure as "King's" Chapel, locals began calling it the "Stone Chapel" instead. President George Washington sat in the old royal governor's pew for a 1789 concert in his honor, a symbolic act whose meaning was lost on no one. Although today a Unitarian church, King's Chapel serves as a tangible reminder of Boston's estrangement from and eventual reconciliation with its English ancestry.

Old Granary Burying Ground

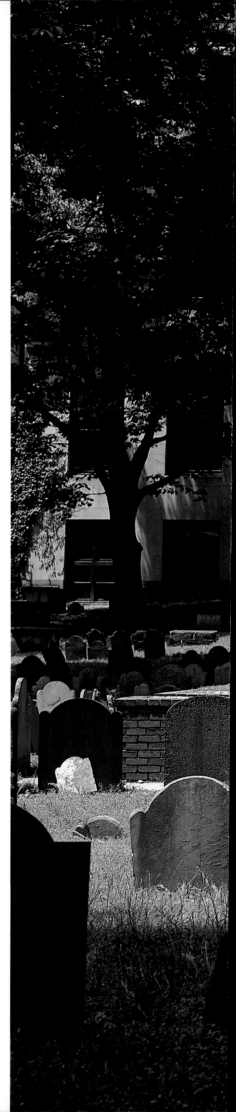

In the Old Granary Burying Ground, the dead do tell tales. Sam Adams, John Hancock, and Crispus Attucks all speak of war and revolution; Peter Faneuil and Paul Revere call attention to ethnic identity, while the Franklin family attests to enduring parental devotion. Many of the headstones chronicle New England's evolving religious values.

The first story Old Granary tells is of Boston's growing population and its struggles against disease in the seventeenth century. Thirty years after the town's founding in 1630, its original burying ground (located next to King's Chapel today) filled up quickly as the first generation of Puritans aged and passed away. To serve those in the central and southerly end of town, local officials in 1660 created the Old Granary Burying Ground on what was then the northeast corner of Boston Common. Many of the earliest burial markers were made of wood and have long since disappeared, leaving John Wakefield's 1667 tombstone as the oldest in the yard.

The curious name for the burying ground originated in the early eighteenth century when the town erected a public granary, hoping that it would prevent the sorts of food shortages and rioting that had plagued the community during Queen Anne's War. The site is now occupied by the beautiful Park Street Church, built in 1809 and mistakenly assumed by visitors to be connected to the graveyard. Another common misconception about the burying ground is that Benjamin Franklin, a Boston native, is buried within its walls. The source of this fallacy is a twenty-one foot obelisk erected to honor his parents, who are interred there.

A number of Franklin's fellow revolutionaries have found their way into Old Granary, however. John Hancock and Samuel Adams, both of whom joined Franklin in signing the Declaration of Independence, are perhaps the best-known patriots buried there, but Robert Treat Paine, James Bowdoin, and Paul Revere are also present.

Boston Athenaeum

Lovers of learning have called 10½ Beacon Street home for over 150 years. Through its doors can be found one of the largest and most prestigious private libraries in the United States, the Boston Athenaeum. Education and literary pursuits had been hallmarks of the community long before the Anthology Society, a gentlemen's social and literary club, opened the Athenaeum on Court Street in 1807. However, there was growing concern that Boston was losing status to other cultural centers in the new nation and that the democratic politics of the era were undermining a classical education. The Athenaeum was designed to remedy this situation by offering its members exclusive access to the finest works of history, literature, and philosophy then available.

The Boston Athenaeum continued to grow with two major renovations to the building in the twentieth century. The first, from 1913 to 1914, added two new floors to the original three-story structure. And in an effort to better preserve fragile volumes, the Athenaeum installed a state-of-the-art climate-control system as part of a $30 million renovation between 1999 and 2002. It has remained vital to the scholarly community not only by modernizing its facilities, but also by specializing in rare and historically valuable art and literature.

Nichols House

Jonathan Mason commissioned architect Charles Bulfinch to design four row houses, 51-57 Mount Vernon Street, as future homes for four of his five daughters in 1804. Mason had once been a law clerk for John Adams.

In 1795, Mason joined with Harrison Gray Otis and several other wealthy Federalist gentlemen to form the Mount Vernon Proprietors, a syndicate that sought to develop the land around Beacon Hill. Plans were then underway to build a new State House nearby, and property values in the area were sure to rise as a result. The Proprietors negotiated the purchase of unimproved land owned by the portrait artist John Singleton Copley, who spent most of his time in England and was largely unaware of Boston's growth. After his agent signed the deed, however, Copley realized his mistake in selling such valuable land and unsuccessfully tried to void the transaction.

Having completed the largest land transfer in Boston's history to that point, the Mount Vernon Proprietors set to work laying out streets and building homes. The original plan called for Mount Vernon Street to feature mansion-houses set back thirty feet from the roadway, and Mason himself was the first to construct such a stately edifice in 1800. But Stephen Higginson Jr. broke the mold in 1803 when he hired Bulfinch to build him a series of row houses that he sold off the next year. Mason quickly followed suit with the houses for his daughters, 51-57 Mount Vernon Street. Of the four buildings, only Number 55 retains much of its original appearance.

Lewis and Harriet Hayden House

Behind the unassuming brick walls of their home on 66 Phillips Street, abolitionists Lewis and Harriet Hayden operated Boston's main depot on the Underground Railroad, earning it affectionate nicknames such as "citadel of liberty" and "temple of refuge." Having escaped bondage in Kentucky, Lewis Hayden empathized with the enslaved and was determined to do everything in his power to liberate them. Twice in the early 1850s, he was arrested and released for his role in plots to free captured fugitives awaiting deportation to the South.

The vitality and leadership of Boston's black community in the fight against slavery had attracted the Haydens to the city in the 1840s. The couple took up residence in the largely African-American neighborhood on the north slope of Beacon Hill. While Lewis opened up a successful used clothing shop on Cambridge Street. They also began hosting abolitionist meetings, and before long their address was closely identified with the antislavery movement. Wendell Phillips, William Lloyd Garrison, Charles Sumner and other leading abolitionists were regular visitors to the home. John Brown of Harper's Ferry fame also regarded him as a close friend and confidante.

Once the Civil War broke out in 1861, Lewis Hayden joined Frederick Douglass in calling for the use of black soldiers and sailors in the military, and he helped recruit elements of the 54th Massachusetts regiment. Hayden believed that the historic sacrifices of African-Americans entitled them to the rights of citizenship.

Edward Hatch Memorial Shell

Warm summer evenings in Boston often bring with them the sounds of outdoor concerts wafting across the waters of the Charles River from the nearby Hatch Memorial Shell. Erected in 1940 as a gift from the estate of Maria Hatch, the 40-foot high band shell (named in honor of her late brother) fronts a two-acre lawn that provides a leisurely atmosphere for taking in all sorts of cultural activities. Easily the most popular is the annual Fourth of July extravaganza featuring fireworks and performances by the Boston Pops Orchestra, which routinely draws hundreds of thousands from New England and beyond. But public concerts in the park could be heard as far back as the 1910s, shortly after completion of what was then called the Embankment, a promenade overlooking the scenic Charles River Basin. Now known as the Esplanade, the area was improved in the late 1920s through the philanthropy of Helen Osbourne Storrow and became a fashionable retreat for Beacon Hill and Back Bay residents. A young Arthur Fiedler brought the Boston Pops to the Esplanade in the summer of 1929, marking the beginning of a longstanding tradition.

Today the Hatch Memorial Shell is more popular than ever. Beyond the Pops, the site plays host to jazz festivals, rhythm and blues acts, rock groups, and reggae bands among others.

African Meeting House

Since abolitionist William Lloyd Garrison described it in 1832 as an "obscure schoolhouse," the African Meeting House has become a national landmark and a major attraction on Boston's popular Black Heritage Trail. Brought together by the end of slavery in the state and continued discrimination from whites, Boston's black population increasingly congregated on the north side of Beacon Hill after the Revolution. There they built the African Meeting House in 1806 as a place where they could freely gather to worship, to educate and entertain each other, and to push for political reform in the new nation.

The meetinghouse proved priceless to Boston's black community. No longer forced to endure segregation at white churches or to borrow space at Faneuil Hall, they could enjoy the sermons of Baptist minister Thomas Paul in the upstairs hall. Downstairs they set up a school for their children, who were as yet unwelcome at local white schools.

The post-Civil War period saw Boston's black population shift away from Beacon Hill toward the South End and even into neighboring Roxbury, which, along with the successful abolition of slavery in 1865, reduced the role of the African Meeting House in the community. At the same time, growing numbers of Jewish immigrants began moving into the area and purchased the building for a synagogue, a function it performed for most of the twentieth century. In 1972, however, the newly founded Museum of Afro-American History in Boston purchased the building and reclaimed it as part of the nation's black heritage.

Massachusetts General Hospital

Few institutions have proven more vital to Boston's development over the past two centuries than Massachusetts General Hospital. Founded in 1811, it is the oldest and largest hospital in New England, performing tens of thousands of surgeries every year and employing more workers than any nongovernmental agency in the city. Its cutting-edge research facilities reflect the hospital's historic and enduring relationship with the Harvard Medical School, and its commitment to innovative healthcare is evident in a research budget that annually exceeds $200 million. Progressive treatment methods contribute to Massachusetts General's reputation as one of the leading hospitals in the United States.

A major medical advance for which the hospital can claim credit is the first successful use of anesthesia in the operating room. Dr. William Morton had previously applied ether to his dental patients before offering it to Dr. John C. Warren, chief surgeon and co-founder of Massachusetts General Hospital, to help remove a tumor from the jaw of Gilbert Abbott in 1846.

News of the event thrilled the medical community, prompting one doctor to declare, "every one who has any sympathy for human suffering must rejoice in the discovery." The operation has been memorialized on a monument located in the Public Garden, but what has been largely forgotten was the subsequent battle over credit and reward for the discovery.

In spite of triumphs such as the discovery of anesthesia, some Bostonians cast a suspicious eye on the research being done for Massachusetts General in the 1830s and 1840s. Rumors were rife that so-called "resurrection men" were hired to secretly exhume bodies for use at the Boston Medical College next to the hospital. And when Dr. George Parkman went missing in 1849 only to be found murdered at the college, presumably at the hands of Dr. John Webster, the news led to rioting outside the hospital grounds. Massachusetts General and the Medical College survived the scandal, however, and during the Civil War provided emergency services for the Union cause. Since then the hospital has acquired a reputation as a world-class facility.

Back Bay

Previous page: Swan Boats on Public Garden Lagoon.

Public Garden: George Washington Equestrian Statue

Thomas Ball's 1869 equestrian statue of George Washington in Boston's Public Garden reflects the mood of the post-Civil War period, when a bloodied nation craving peace and unity anxiously turned to its Founders for strength and reassurance. Unveiled for the Fourth of July, Ball's remains the most beloved of the three Washington statues erected in Boston. Washington cuts a commanding figure in his military uniform, sitting over thirty feet above the ground astride his bronze mount and atop a granite foundation. He commanded the army that drove the King's troops out of Boston during the Revolutionary War, an event still celebrated every March 17th as Evacuation Day. Ironically, his statue stands not far from where British soldiers had embarked upon their fateful march to Lexington and Concord in 1775.

The sculpture's appeal is surely enhanced by its verdant surroundings. Although botanical gardens had existed on the site since the 1830s, the Public Garden was just coming into its own when Ball's statue debuted in 1869. The area had been little more than a marshy tidal basin when Washington knew the city in the 1770s. But Boston's increasingly urban character in the antebellum era put pressure on the community to fill the Back Bay for land development. Instead of smelly mudflats, which they worried would compromise people's health, a few influential inhabitants envisioned fragrant flowers. Led by Horace Gray, a wealthy industrialist and avid gardener, they joined together in 1837 and created a botanical garden complete with a conservatory. A favorite retreat for locals and tourists alike on warm, sunny days, the Garden features a man-made pond where one can board one of Boston's famed Swan Boats for a leisurely cruise.

WASHINGTON

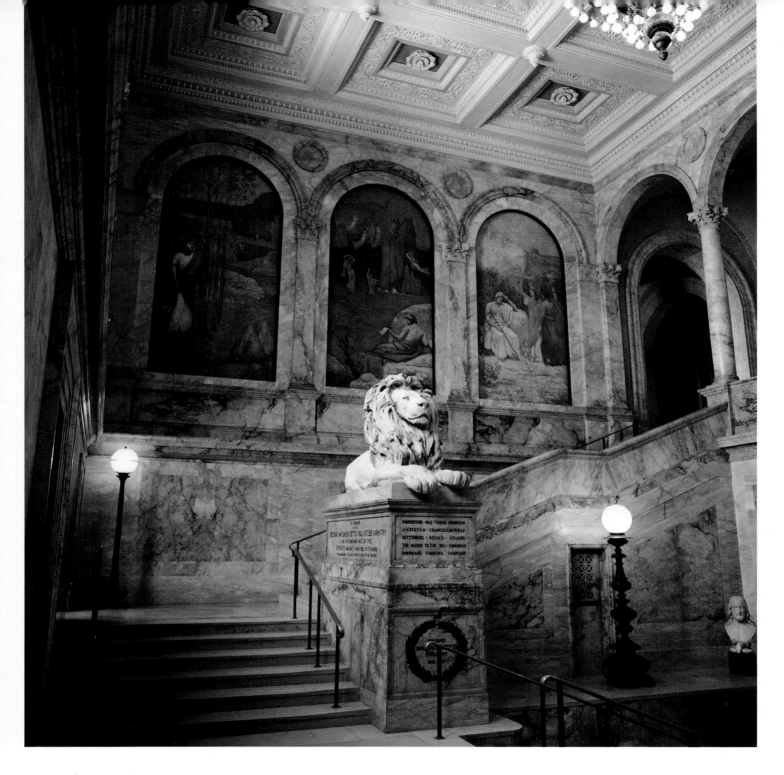

Boston Public Library

If H.H. Richardson's Trinity Church has an architectural equal in Boston, it would be its Copley Square neighbor, the Boston Public Library. Opened in 1895, the building came with a staggering $2.5 million price tag, which today seems a small price to pay for masterpieces by some of the era's best architects, sculptors, and artists. The intent of the library was to celebrate and inspire the advancement of learning not only through the books on the shelves, but also the paintings on the walls and even the walls themselves. Several architects were turned down before the library's trustees found someone who shared their bold vision, Charles Follen McKim of the renowned New York firm of McKim, Mead, and White.

No one disputed the fact that Boston needed a new public library by the 1880s. The original library had been founded in the early 1850s after city officials threatened to appropriate the Boston Athenaeum's private holdings for public use. Unwilling to see their exclusive society opened to the masses, yet believing in the value of libraries for shaping popular values, members of the Athenaeum were active in the creation of a public library. The Boston Public Library was the first of its kind in any major American city.

The city's growing ethnic and religious diversity in the post-Civil War period concerned the self-proclaimed guardians of Boston's cultural traditions, the so-called Brahmins, who feared that their influence was waning. Rather than edifying themselves at the library, immigrants and working-class poor seemed to prefer the conviviality of neighborhood taverns. To counteract this apparent trend, some local leaders proposed moving the Boston Public Library to the spacious Back Bay, where many Brahmin families were relocating, and transforming it into a monument to civic improvement. They also saw the new library as continuing a tradition of public education that connected them to their Puritan ancestors. To promote the project, the state legislature in 1880 donated land on the corner of Boylston and Dartmouth with the provision that work on the site begin within three years, an offer that was extended after trustees initially failed to find a suitable architect.

The cornerstone of McKim's building was laid on November 28, 1888. His light, classical design for the library contrasted with the dark, medieval look of many surrounding structures on Copley Square, but he persuaded skeptics that they could coexist.

Opposite: Connecting the Library's Entrance Hall with the Main Staircase is a deep triumphal arch. The marble of the steps is ivory gray Echaillon, mottled with fossil shells; that of the walls is a richly variegated yellow Siena. The great twin lions, couchant, on pedestals at the turn of the stairs are of unpolished Siena marble and are the work of Louis St. Gaudens. They are memorials to Massachusetts Civil War infantry regiments, the Second and the Twentieth.

Right: The two large statues on the platform in front of the Library represent Art and Science. These were sculpted by the Boston artist Bela Pratt and were set in place in 1912.

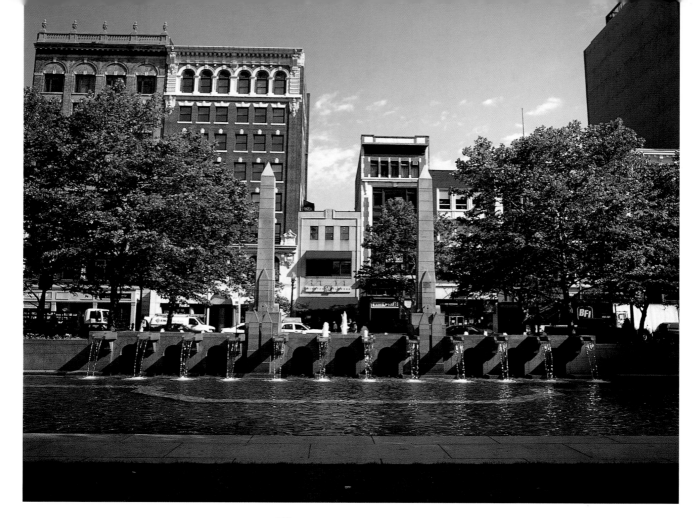

Copley Square

Lovers of architecture recognize Copley Square as the address of Boston's most treasured buildings. Sports fans know it best as the celebrated finish line for the Boston Marathon.

Originally called Art Square, Copley Square emerged in the 1880s at the awkward juncture of the South End and Back Bay landfill projects. As Huntington Avenue headed northeast out of the South End toward Back Bay, it cut diagonally across St. James and Boylston, creating two triangular plots of land. The undeveloped site had hosted the 1869 National Peace Jubilee, which featured various entertainments in an enormous, though temporary, Coliseum. Two years later, Trinity Church purchased the eastern triangle to build H.H. Richardson's grand structure for the congregation.

The Museum of Fine Arts briefly joined Trinity Church on the southerly portion of the square before moving elsewhere and being replaced by the Copley Plaza Hotel in 1913. A more permanent resident arrived in 1895 with the opening of the Boston Public Library.

By the middle of the twentieth century, Copley Square had lost some of its charm. Traffic through the area had increased markedly, making it noisier and more dangerous for pedestrians. The S.S. Pierce Building, erected in 1887 for the popular grocer, was torn down in 1958 to create parking space on the southwest corner of Copley Square.

In 1965, city officials chose the architectural firm of Sasaski and Associates to redesign Copley Square and give it a modern look. The Huntington Avenue traverse was removed entirely, which eliminated automobile traffic through the square. The architects installed a series of concrete steps and landings that gradually led to a sunken fountain and pool along Boylston Street. The intent of this design was twofold: 1) to inversely complement the towering Trinity Church nearby, and 2) to drop the park below street level and create an oasis from the hustle-and-bustle of the city. Virtually the entire square was paved over, with the exception of some perimeter areas where Crab Apples, Honey Locusts, and other types of trees were planted.

St. Botolph Club

What do poet Robert Frost, historian Francis Parkman, sculptor Daniel Chester French, and artist John Singer Sargent have in common? All were once members of the exclusive St. Botolph Club, Boston's premier social and literary society for over a century. Named after the seventh-century English abbot from whom Boston also derived its name, the Club was founded in 1880 to encourage the arts and maintain Boston's literary reputation. Its founders were drawn from the ranks of the Boston Brahmins, the city's self-appointed cultural guardians, and although membership has diversified over the years the Club remains dedicated to its original mission.

In recent years, St. Botolph has struggled to keep itself relevant in artistic circles and to maintain the respect of the local community. Opportunities abound elsewhere for talented writers, composers, and painters, many of whom view private clubs as passé. In 2000, the Club took a step forward and elected its first female president, retired MIT professor Irene Tayler.

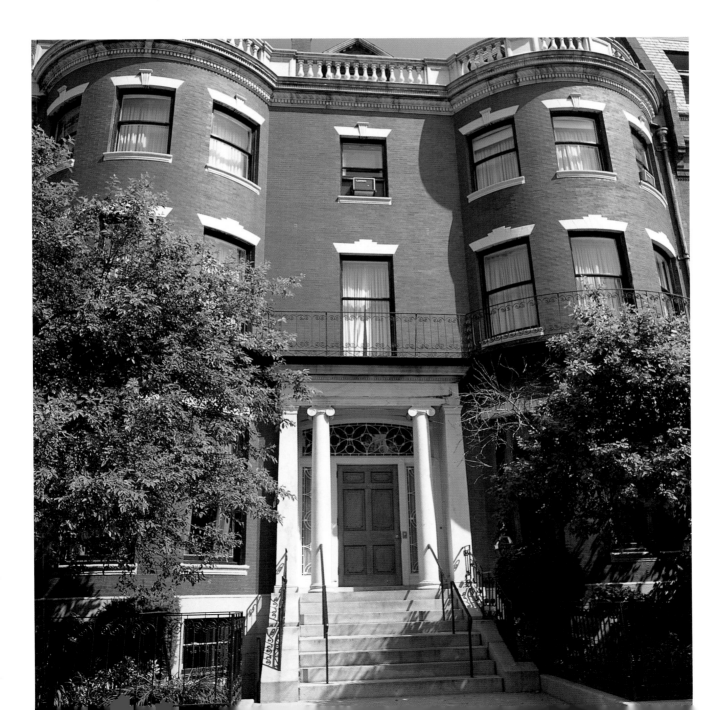

John Hancock Tower

Before the Big Dig boondoggle, there was the Hancock Tower hullabaloo. Boston's tallest building was born of a corporate rivalry between two insurance giants in the 1960s, the hometown John Hancock Company and the New Jersey-based Prudential. Feeling overshadowed by the massive, fifty-two story Prudential Center after its completion in 1965, executives at Hancock announced plans to build their own, larger skyscraper nearby.

Unfortunately, there was a public outcry after construction got underway in 1968. The tons of earth removed to prepare the structure's foundation inadvertently caused settling in the surrounding soil and damaged neighboring buildings, sidewalks, and underground cables. Not only did the problem spark rumors that the Hancock Tower might sink, but it also led to lawsuits that cost the company millions of dollars. The tendency of the sixty-story building to sway excessively in strong winds also unnerved some of its first tenants until the problem was dealt with at a cost of three million additional dollars. Of all the hazards associated with the Hancock Tower's early years, however, only one became so infamous that it lives on in local lore- the problem of falling glass. Even today, some who remember the incident cannot help casting a quick glance skyward as they walk past the building, although the problem has long since been resolved.

Despite construction flaws, mounting expenses, repeated delays, and intense public scrutiny of the project, company officials persevered, and on September 29, 1976 the new John Hancock Building was formally dedicated. The shimmering tower of glass quickly silenced its critics and soon began garnering praise for its bold, innovative design. Decades after its controversial construction, Bostonians have become very protective of a building that to many symbolizes the historic city's continuing vitality in the twenty-first century.

Newbury Street

With its upscale shopping and celebrity appeal, Newbury Street is Boston's answer to New York's Fifth Avenue. Yet the charming Victorian brownstones that house many of its boutiques lend Newbury Street a style all of its own, one that recalls its days as a fashionable residential address for the Boston Brahmins. Outdoor cafés, street musicians, and sidewalk art all add to the cosmopolitan character of the place, where one can find everything from Parisian handbags to Indian cuisine. The intimacy of its shops also provide a nice contrast to the crowds that dominate other popular shopping districts such as Quincy Market and Copley Place.

Newbury Street is more than a shopper's paradise, however. It has a rich architectural heritage as well. Since the 1960s, it has been home to the Boston Architectural Center, founded in the 1880s as a club for professional and student architects. The Neo-Gothic Church of the Covenant, located on the corner of Newbury and Berkeley Streets, boasts Boston's tallest steeple and one the largest collections of liturgical Tiffany windows in the country. Inside Emmanuel Episcopal Church, the Leslie Lindsey Memorial Chapel honors a young newlywed who perished with her husband aboard the ill-fated *Lusitania* in 1915. For scholars and genealogists, the major attraction on Newbury Street is the New England Historic Genealogical Society, which contains family records dating all the way back to the seventeenth century.

Trinity Church

Given Boston's religious origins and rich spiritual heritage, it is rather fitting that a church should be judged its architectural masterpiece. And yet the Episcopal Trinity Church, built between 1873 and 1877, is precisely the kind of structure the Puritan founders would have found abhorrent. They strove for simplicity in their religious meetinghouses, rejecting the elaborate designs of European cathedrals in favor of plain wooden structures. The cosmopolitan tastes of the Anglicans, first evident in King's Chapel and Christ Church (Old North), are often credited with injecting more refinement into local church structure, although the original 1735 Trinity Church had a comparatively uninspiring exterior.

Having survived the Revolution against English authority in the 1770s and 1780s, Trinity thrived in the new republic. Its success as a congregation was manifested in the new, larger and more elaborate Gothic-style church that replaced its predecessor on the Summer Street site in 1829. This solid stone structure existed until November of 1872, when one of the worst fires in Boston's history gutted the building along with hundreds of others in the downtown district. Because the fire began close by, the Trinity congregation had little time to gather up its possessions before the flames engulfed their beloved church.

Trinity Church's highly anticipated dedication in February of 1877 became a community event, attended by scores of clergy as well as both the Governor of Massachusetts and the Mayor of Boston.

Ever innovative, church leaders embarked on a new effort in 2002 to create a geothermal heat exchange that warms the building's basement, creating more usable space for the large congregation. The project is part of an ongoing, multi-million dollar renovation that also includes restoration of ceiling murals, stained-glass windows, and the church's organ.

Old South Church

The construction of Cummings and Sears's magnificent 1875 Italian Gothic church was a bittersweet moment for both the Old South Church congregation and Bostonians generally. For over two hundred years, the congregation had worshipped at their comparatively modest meetinghouse on Washington Street, which had worked its way deep into their hearts. Families that had for generations lived nearby were now moving to the more fashionable Back Bay. The streets surrounding the old meetinghouse were becoming so crowded with commercial traffic and questionable characters that, as church leaders complained, "it is hardly a suitable place for females to walk in the evening." A major fire that devastated the city and damaged the Old

South Meetinghouse in 1872 convinced many congregants that the time was right for a move. Although the move was unpopular with some members, construction of Old South's beautiful new Back Bay church got underway in 1872. When it was finished three years later, even critics begrudgingly admired its architecture. The brown, gray, and pink hues of its stonework proved irresistibly charming, and its 246-foot bell tower made it an instant landmark.

While their proud heritage remains, Old South has moved forward as a congregation. In 2005, Nancy S. Taylor became the first female minister in the church's 336-year history, a milestone that reflects the congregation's commitment to inclusiveness. Her progressive policies suggest that Old South will continue to be a leader in the future as it has been in the past. "[Old South] made trouble getting the Boston Tea Party started so many years ago," she proudly proclaims. "And we're going to keep getting into just that kind of trouble."

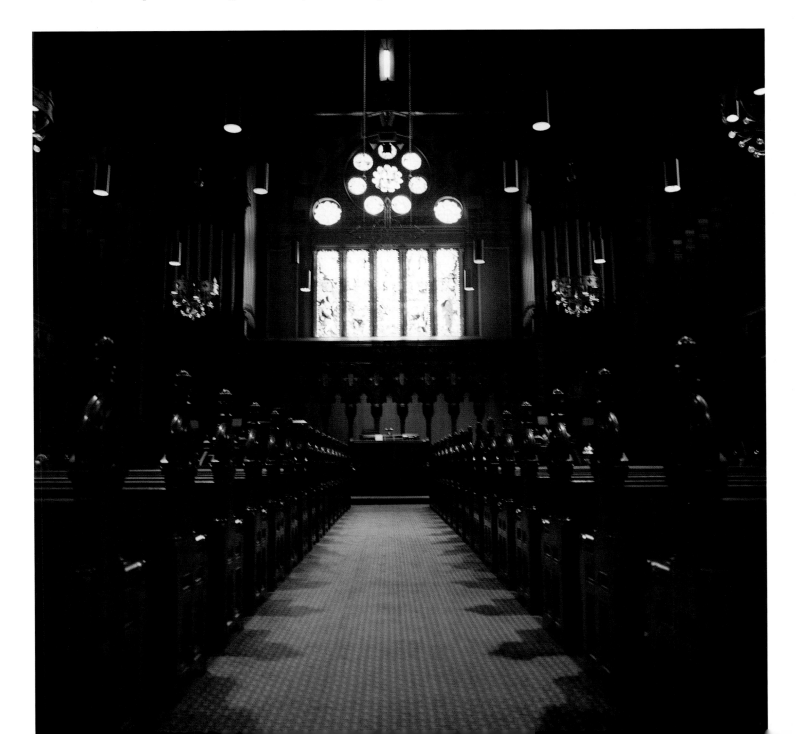

Boston Women's Memorial

The 2003 dedication of the Women's Memorial on the Commonwealth Avenue Mall capped a decade-long effort to correct the glaring gender imbalance in Boston's public art. In a city filled with commemorative sculptures, only two previous works had featured women—the statues of Anne Hutchinson and Mary Dyer on the grounds of the State House. Yet even these figures were cast primarily as seventeenth-century religious martyrs rather than as representatives of their gender.

The movement to better recognize women's accomplishments was spearheaded by Stella Trafford, the long-time chair of the Commonwealth Avenue Mall Committee, along with the city's Women's Commission. A task force composed of historians, artists, and interested Back Bay residents was created to launch fundraisers, search for a sculptor, and consider

Houses along Commonwealth Avenue Mall.

designs for the monument. Response from the community was generally positive, and over $425,000 was raised from public and private donors for the project.

While the memorial has proved very popular as part of the Boston Women's Heritage Trail, it has had detractors. Some wondered whether a city already littered with monuments really needed another; perhaps they could be combined together into a giant Memorial to Everybody, one local quipped. Bergmann's bronze monument has even been compared, perhaps unfairly, to such masterpieces as Saint-Gaudens's Shaw Memorial on the Common and found wanting. Judging by all the attention, however, Bergmann and the Memorial Committee achieved their goal of raising public awareness about women's contributions to American society.

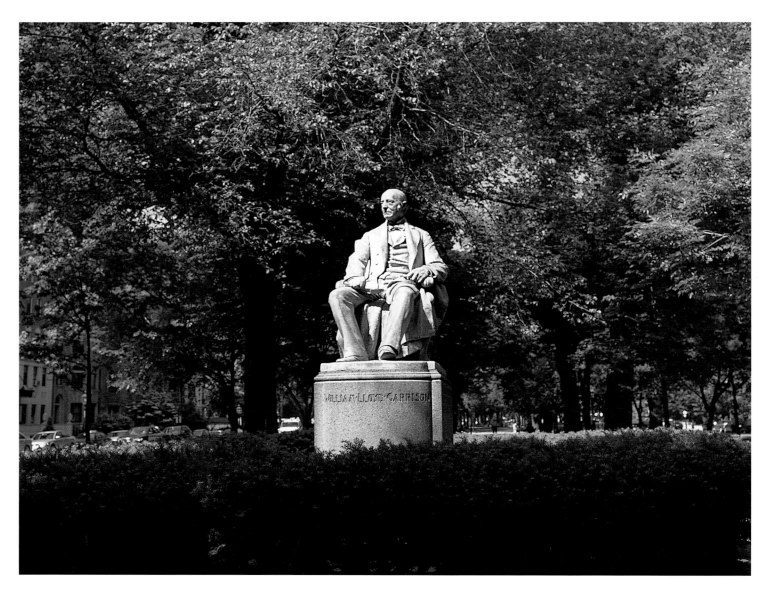

William Lloyd Garrison Statue

Sitting uncharacteristically quiet on the Commonwealth Avenue Mall is William Lloyd Garrison, the vocal abolitionist leader whose words stirred the conscience of a nation. "I am in earnest," he proclaimed from the pages of his anti-slavery newspaper the *Liberator*, "I will not equivocate—I will not excuse—I will not retreat a single inch—AND I *WILL* BE HEARD." Many white Bostonians in the 1830s did not particularly like what they heard from Garrison, who criticized both church and state for complicity with slaveholders, and in 1835 a mob dragged him through the streets in an effort to silence him. It is a testament to how much the city had changed that less than a decade after his death in 1879, Garrison's statue was dedicated on the Mall. Sculpted by Olin Levi Warner, the monument depicts a dignified, yet determined Garrison sitting forward with papers clutched in his hand. Near his feet sit bound volumes of the *Liberator*, and inscribed around the memorial are both his famed declaration of activism and his assertion of universal brotherhood: "My country is the world. My countrymen are all mankind." Garrison's rhetoric still has the power to inspire those who stop to contemplate his statue. At the height of the Cold War and the Civil Rights movement, President John F. Kennedy credited the Garrison memorial with strengthening his own political convictions.

Bull & Finch Pub

The Bull & Finch Pub on Beacon Street may be the place "where everybody knows your name," but most people recognize the bar by its more familiar television moniker, Cheers. The original name was a clever play on the surname of architect Charles Bulfinch, who designed many of Beacon Hill's finest homes in the early nineteenth century. For over a decade after its 1969 opening, the Bull & Finch operated as an English-style pub patronized mostly by locals. All that changed in the early 1980s, after a visit from television producer Glen Charles led to the pub's likeness being featured in a new sitcom called *Cheers*.

Fans of *Cheers* are often disappointed to find that the interior of the real Bull & Finch is not identical to the Hollywood set. The major difference, besides the absence of such memorable characters as Sam, Norm, and Frasier, is the use of a wall bar instead of the island bar that appears on the show. Yet a closer look reveals many similarities, from the cigar-store Indian inside the door to the style of the windows and seats. During the show's heyday, those seats became notoriously difficult to get.

Boston's affection for the show was never more apparent than in 1993, when it was announced that *Cheers* would end its remarkable run on May 20th. Governor William Weld declared the day "*Cheers* Day" in Massachusetts, and cast members were invited to the Bull & Finch to celebrate. While they joined local sports legends and politicians for drinks inside the bar, out on the Common a giant screen was set up for Bostonians to enjoy the show's final episode together. Temporary bleachers were also erected in front of the pub so fans could watch a live airing of the "Tonight Show with Jay Leno" and join in for one last rendition of *Cheers's* catchy theme song.

The Bull & Finch Pub is still basking in the afterglow of *Cheers* years after the Hollywood spotlight has faded. Although business slowed a bit in the late 1990s and following the terrorist attacks of 9/11, the bar is still a "must-see" for many visitors to the city. In 2001, Kershaw responded to their demands for "authenticity" by replicating the show's set at a second location in Faneuil Hall Marketplace. He also officially renamed the Beacon Hill bar "Cheers," much to the delight of tourists confused by its original name. Thanks to Kershaw's marketing and the show's syndication, the pub should remain a Boston landmark for generations to come.

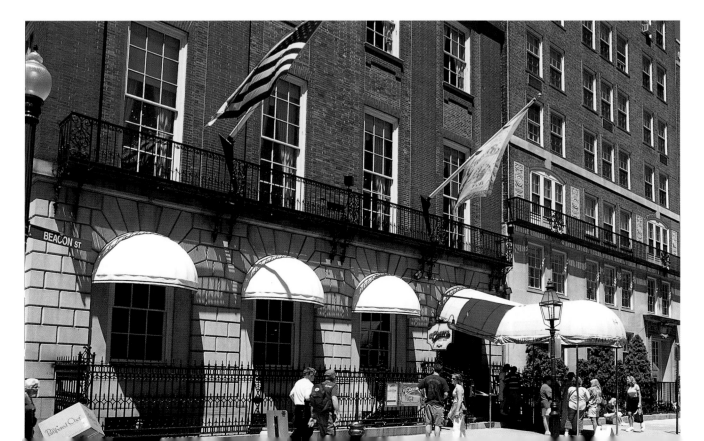

Gibson House Museum

Once the proud cultural elite of the community, Boston's Brahmin families, which Oliver Wendell Holmes famously described as a "harmless, inoffensive, untitled aristocracy," had come to seem strangely old-fashioned by the early twentieth century. Indeed, when Charles Hammond Gibson, Jr. proposed that his family's home at 137 Beacon Street be maintained as a museum to exhibit the city's fading Victorian customs, even relatives scoffed at the suggestion. But the unconventional Gibson persisted, convinced that someday people would again appreciate the Victorian era. Decades after his death in 1954, the verdict on that prediction is still out. Although Gibson's 1860 brownstone townhouse has been recognized as a National Historic Landmark, visitors to the city often overlook his museum despite its rich collections and quirky history.

The filling and development of Back Bay, where the Gibson House resides, dominated the last half of the nineteenth century and transformed the area from a muddy, smelly wasteland into the new heart of the city. Attracted by this "New Land" and disturbed by the flood of Irish immigrants settling into older neighborhoods, Brahmin families sought refuge in the Back Bay. Gibson's wealthy, widowed grandmother moved her family into their new home in 1860, making them among the first to relocate. The house featured many modern conveniences of the era, including indoor plumbing and gas lighting. Redecorated in the 1880s to reflect the latest fashions, the home still possesses many fine examples of period furniture, wallpapers, and textiles.

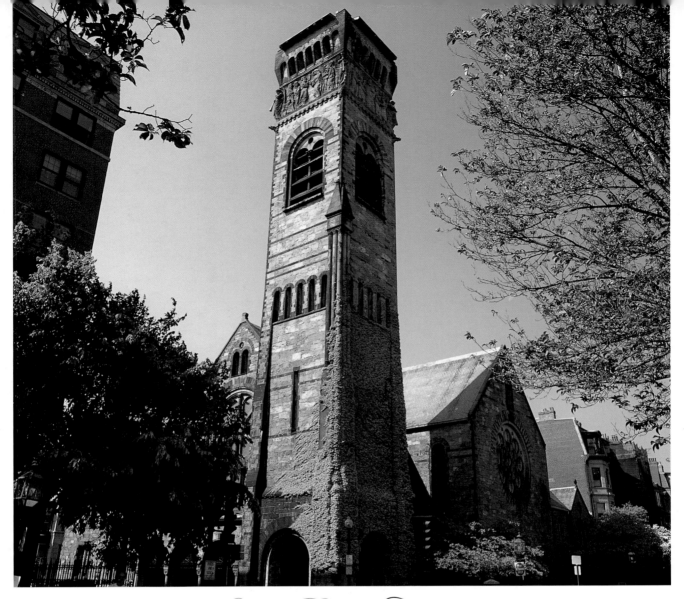

First Baptist Church

The First Baptist Church on Commonwealth
Avenue is a source of immense pride for a
congregation that once worshipped secretly for
fear of persecution. Boston's Puritans, determined to create a holy commonwealth, had little
tolerance for Baptists, whose unorthodox practice of adult baptism they considered heresy. Yet
despite the threat of imprisonment, corporeal
punishment, and banishment, a few committed
Baptists met behind closed doors in the 1660s to
follow their consciences.

Pressure from English officials in the 1670s
and 1680s forced local authorities to relax their
policies against nonconformists, enabling the
Baptists to erect a small meetinghouse near the
water in Boston's congested North End. The spot
not only facilitated their baptismal rites, but also
placed them closer to many of the laboring-class
families they serviced. Those who lived on the

political and economic margins of the community appreciated the Baptists' inclusiveness, and
the church grew so quickly that a second, larger
meetinghouse replaced the original in the early
eighteenth century.

First Baptist gradually migrated westward as
both it and the city expanded in the nineteenth
century. Having built themselves a more
refined brick church a few streets over from
their original North End location, the congregation sold their colonial meetinghouse to
another Baptist group in 1829. This was
followed by another shift onto Somerset Street
near Beacon Hill. Each move placed the
once-shunned Baptists closer to circles of
respectability in the community. The coup in
this sense was the acquisition of the church on
fashionable Commonwealth Avenue in 1882.

North End and Charlestown

Paul Revere House

"Listen, my children, and you shall hear/ Of the midnight ride of Paul Revere...." So begins Henry Wadsworth Longfellow's famous 1860 poem about the Boston silversmith turned Revolutionary patriot, Paul Revere. On the night of April 18, 1775, Revere left his home and family on 19 Court Square to warn the Massachusetts countryside about an impending British march against rebel munitions at Concord. "You know the rest. In the books you have read/ How the British regulars fired and fled—/ How the farmers gave them ball for ball,/ From behind each fence and farm-yard wall." The Revolutionary War had begun.

Today the Paul Revere House has the unique distinction of being downtown Boston's only remaining seventeenth-century dwelling, its survival owing as much to Longfellow's celebrated poem as to Revere's residence. In fact, Revere was not even the original owner of the house, which was built for Robert Howard about 1680. The house's traditional post-and-beam design was already falling out of fashion by the time Revere bought it in 1770.

Revere's political activities on behalf of the patriot cause in the 1760s and 1770s also kept him away from his trade as a silversmith and engraver, although he sometimes turned his skills toward producing anti-British propaganda. The two most famous examples are his 1768 "Sons of Liberty" punchbowl and his 1770 engraving depicting the Boston Massacre. Revere's outrage over the massacre, in which five civilians were killed during a confrontation with the King's troops, was on display at his Court Square home the following year as well. As part of the first annual commemoration of the event, he constructed silhouettes portraying the massacre and placed them before his windows for everyone to see. Such behavior did not endear Revere to royalist authorities, but it did earn him the respect of patriot leaders, for whom he acted as a valuable liaison with local artisans and other communities. Still, his efforts would not win him lasting fame until Longfellow's patriotic poem, written decades after Revere's death, stirred the imagination of Northerners preparing to defend the Union in the Civil War.

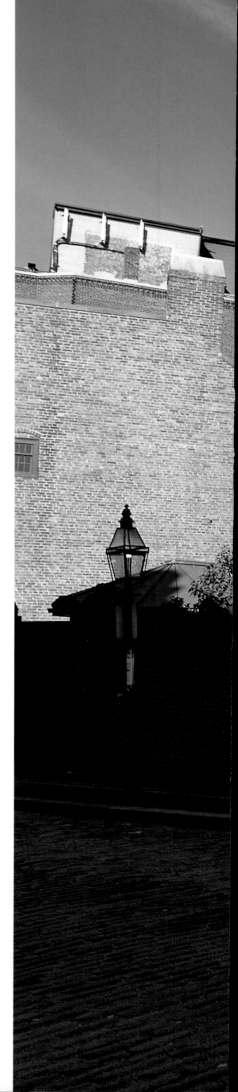

Previous page: North End Church in the North End.

Sacred Heart Church

The Sacred Heart Catholic Church has been the heart and soul of Boston's Italian community for well over a century, but its once strong, steady pulse has recently weakened as both the North End and the Catholic Church change around it. Even before the arrival of Italian immigrants in the late nineteenth century, the North Square site possessed a spiritual quality about it, serving as a seamen's bethel where transient sailors could go to worship and remember friends who had perished at sea.

Despite religious ties to other immigrant groups, Italians settling in the North End after the Civil War wanted their own place of worship, where priests spoke their language and shared their cultural values. They built their first church, St. Leonard of Port Maurice, on the corner of Hanover and Prince Street in 1876. But tensions within the congregation, whose members came from different regions of Italy, caused a split that resulted in the creation of Sacred Heart.

Widely regarded as a cornerstone of the North End's Italian community, its sentimental importance has grown even as its congregation dwindled in recent years. Immigration from Italy has slowed, and many older residents with ties to the homeland have died. The younger generation is being pushed out of the North End by rising property values as other Bostonians rediscover the neighborhood's Old World charm, which is ironically being lost in the process. Sacred Heart now stands as one of the last remaining connections to the way the community once was.

Paul Revere Mall and North End Church.

Old North (Christ) Church

It is rather ironic that a church so thoroughly identified with American independence should be affiliated with the Church of England. Christ Church, or, as it is more commonly called, Old North Church, reflected the expansion of the Anglican faith in eighteenth-century Boston. Having recently received protection against Puritan persecution through a new royal charter, Massachusetts Anglicans felt at liberty to worship openly. By 1722, King's Chapel in Boston could no longer contain its congregation, prompting the purchase of land in the North End for a new church.

In later years, the American Revolution deeply divided members of the congregation, some of whom agreed with Rector Mather Byles that loyalty to the Crown was both a political and religious duty. But incidents such as the Boston Massacre had convinced many otherwise. In the spring of 1775, as tensions in the city mounted, patriot leaders recruited the disgruntled church sexton, Robert Newman, to assist them in alerting neighboring Charlestown if the British began to move on the countryside. The Christ Church steeple was (and still is) easily visible across the Charles River, making it an ideal means of signaling trouble. Trouble came on the night of April 18, when Paul Revere informed Newman that British troops were gathering near Boston Common to be ferried across the river. Eluding the officers lodging at his family's North End home, Newman went directly to the church and quietly unlocked its door with his key. Once inside, he grabbed a pair of lanterns that he had earlier prepared for the occasion and began ascending the narrow, winding staircase to the top of the steeple, where he (and perhaps another church member, John Pulling) briefly lit them to warn of the impending march. Some soldiers nearly nabbed Newman as he left the building, but he snuck out a sanctuary window and safely avoided capture. General Thomas Gage, who worshipped at Christ Church during the British occupation, suspected an inside job and had Newman arrested, although he was later released due to lack of evidence.

Newman's deeds would go unrecognized outside of Boston until immortalized in Henry Wadsworth Longfellow's 1860 poem "Paul Revere's Ride," which unfortunately fails to refer to the sexton by name.

Bunker Hill Monument

Charlestown's majestic Bunker Hill Monument, actually situated on nearby Breed's Hill, honors one of the worst cases of mistaken identity in American history, the so-called Battle of Bunker Hill on June 17, 1775. Why the Americans chose to fortify Breed's Hill rather than the taller Bunker's Hill is unclear. Perhaps Colonel William Prescott's men confused the neighboring hills in the darkness as they occupied the strategic ground overlooking British-occupied Boston. The next day, the colonists repulsed two British attacks before being forced to retreat for lack of ammunition. Some British officers afterwards belittled the American effort, arguing that anyone could have defended such a strong position.

The Americans, of course, saw it differently. They lost the hill, but they gained the confidence that they could stand up to the mighty British army. The Continental Congress sent George Washington to take charge of the troops, and by March of 1776 they had driven the British out of Boston.

The 221-foot-tall Egyptian obelisk that dominates the spot of the battlefield was begun in 1825 as part of the fiftieth anniversary of the battle. Despite such a celebrated beginning, the granite monument took nearly twenty years to finish due to lack of funds. But for the philanthropy of industrialist Amos Lawrence and the Jewish merchant Judah Touro, the monument might never have been completed. Once finished, however, it became as popular a tourist site in the nineteenth century as it is today. "You clamber up three hundred steps to the top," recalled Russian traveler Aleksandr Lakier, who visited the monument in 1857, "but you absolutely forget your fatigue when you reach the summit and there, spread out before your eyes, is a vast panorama of the sea, the naval dockyard, and the piers for ships of various companies and countries." The scenery has certainly changed since Lakier's visit, but the monument still offers one of the better views of Boston.

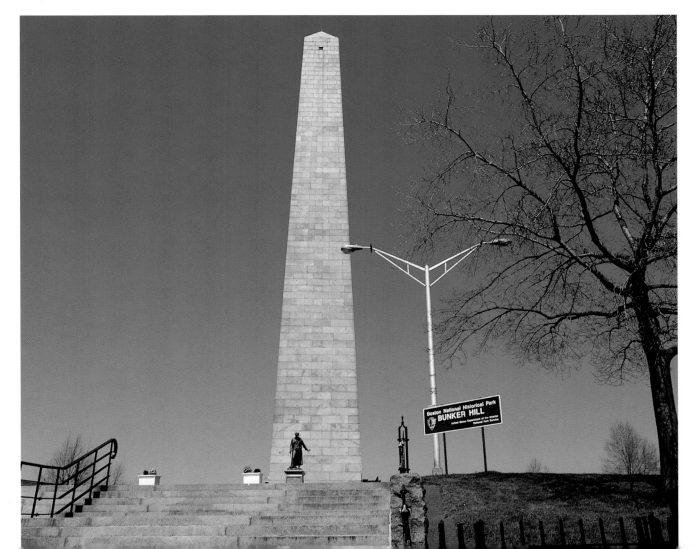

U.S.S. Constitution

Dubbed "Old Ironsides", for its unusually strong oak hull, the U.S.S. *Constitution* is the United States' oldest fully commissioned naval vessel, dating back to 1797. The successful revolution against Britain meant that Americans could no longer rely on the Royal Navy to protect their maritime trade. Especially worrisome were the Barbary pirates, who made a living plundering foreign ships off the North African coast. Relations with France also deteriorated in the 1790s as America's erstwhile ally descended into civil war and revolution. In response to such international threats, Congress authorized the construction of several new frigates for its fledgling navy in 1794, including the *Constitution*—named in honor of the new system of federal government.

The *Constitution* was built at Edmund Harrt's shipyard in Boston's North End, as the Charlestown Navy Yard, where it now resides, was not established until 1800. The ship's legendary strength was the result of an innovative framing design that featured live oak, a denser, more rot-resistant type of wood found in the American South. Its sturdy mainmast, which measured 220 feet high, was made of white pine from Maine, while its planking consisted of white oak. Contrary to popular belief, Paul Revere's Canton Copper Mill

Commandant's House

U.S.S. Constitution

did not produce the sheathing that protected the *Constitution's* hull from worms and barnacles; it was purchased from England.

The *Constitution* and its accompanying museum consistently rank among the most popular sites on Boston's Freedom Trail thanks to their innovative, award-winning approach to education. Hands-on exhibits allow museum visitors to experience many aspects of life on board ship, from firing cannons to napping in a sailor's hammock. The 1805 Commandant's House, with its elegant interior and spectacular view of Boston Harbor, is also open seasonally to the public and available for private functions.

Saint Stephen's Roman Catholic Church

Saint Stephen's is best known as the last remaining church designed by famed Boston architect Charles Bulfinch, although he would have recognized it as the New North Church. Formed in 1714, the Puritan congregation built its first meetinghouse on North Street, not far from the wharves and shipyards where a number of its members worked. Less than a decade later the young church was embroiled in a major controversy over the ordination of Peter Thatcher as assistant minister. Against the advice of many colleagues, the talented Thatcher abandoned his Weymouth flock in 1720 for the more prestigious position in Boston, which some at New North considered unfair and inappropriate. Tempers flared and resulted in part of the congregation leaving to organize a new church several blocks away.

The resilient congregation would weather other storms, including the disruptions of the Revolution, and in 1802 hired Charles Bulfinch to build them a larger, more modern meeting-house on Hanover Street. The cornerstone of New North was laid on September 23, 1802, and where possible Bulfinch used timber from the old wooden meetinghouse for his largely brick and stone building.

Under the leadership of the Reverend Francis Parkman, father of the renowned historian, New North flourished for decades and joined several other congregations in embracing Unitarianism. But the development of the fashionable Back Bay and the influx of Irish Catholic immigrants to the North End after mid-century prompted many of the congregants to leave the declining church, which was sold to the Catholic Diocese in 1862 for $35,000. Renamed Saint Stephen's Church, the largely Irish parish put its own touches on the building, including removal of the weathervane and the addition of a cross.

Tourists often overlook the historic church, distracted either by Cyrus Dallin's equestrian Paul Revere statue across the street or by the mouth-watering aromas of nearby Italian restaurants.

Copp's Hill Burial Ground

High up on a hill overlooking the Charles River sits one of Boston's oldest graveyards, Copp's Hill Burial Ground. When the Puritan founders arrived in 1630, Shawmut Peninsula, as Boston was then known, was rather hilly, making John Winthrop's vision of a "City Upon a Hill" something more than metaphorical. Nineteenth-century urban "improvements" leveled much of the city, but Copp's Hill in the North End escaped relatively (though not completely) unscathed and remains a good example of Boston's natural terrain.

Before modern buildings enveloped it, the exposed hill was often buffeted by sea breezes that made it an ideal location for a windmill to grind meal. In fact, for much of the seventeenth century locals knew it as Windmill Hill, not Copp's Hill. Its latter name is likely derived from William Copp, a cordwainer or shoemaker who originally owned the land. Responding to the needs of its growing North End community, the town purchased the property and established a burial ground on the site in 1659.

The burial ground is a featured stop on the Freedom Trail because of its many connections to the American Revolution. It is the final resting place of Robert Newman, the Old North Church sexton who lit the lanterns warning of a British march to Concord in 1775. Several men associated with the Boston Tea Party, whose names were meant to remain secret, are also believed to be buried there. It was no secret to royal officials that Captain Daniel Malcomb, a suspected smuggler, was interred at Copp's Hill. His public defiance of customs officers before his North End home in 1766 earned him their undying ire. After he passed away a few years later, British soldiers reportedly used his tombstone for target practice. The marks their musket balls left behind are still visible today. British artillery units also used the strategically placed hill to lob cannonballs across the Charles River during the Battle of Bunker Hill. Such a rich Revolutionary heritage made Copp's Hill the perfect backdrop for Esther Forbes's classic children's tale *Johnny Tremain*.

Leonard P. Zakim Bunker Hill Bridge

Boston's newest landmark is a stylish blend of innovation and tradition, a nod to the city's historic past as it looks forward to the future. Dedicated in October of 2002, the Zakim Bunker Hill Bridge is part of the ongoing Big Dig project, which, when finished, will bury Interstate 93 beneath the city and open up new avenues for pedestrians. Swiss engineer Christian Menn was brought in to design a 10-lane bridge that would funnel traffic over the Charles River and down toward tunnels below Boston's North End, a daunting task brilliantly executed. Mann's unique design also had to consider aesthetics and alewife, a fish closely related to herrings whose migration patterns might have been disrupted by a massive shadow cast across the river. As such, sun holes were installed to allow light to filter through to the waters below. Charlestown's nearby Bunker Hill Monument, which is replicated in the twin towers that loom above the bridge, influenced Menn aesthetically, and his triangular cable structure reminds many of the sailing ships that once dominated Boston Harbor. Not everyone approved of its $100 million design, but the sleek bridge with the awkward name quickly won over the community and has become an instant icon.

The bridge's connection to Charlestown and its Revolutionary heritage led members of the local historical society to suggest the name Bunker Hill Bridge. Yet over on Beacon Hill, the Governor's office announced that it should instead be named in honor of the late Leonard P. Zakim, regional director of the Anti-Defamation League. Zakim's tireless efforts on behalf of civil rights were already legendary before his premature death in 1999, and many felt the bridge was symbolic of his work in bridging differences between peoples and faiths. Besides, they reasoned, the Revolutionary War patriots already had a fitting tribute to their sacrifices. Defenders of the Bunker Hill name shot back that the bridge's significance was too great to be dedicated to just one person and that Zakim should be honored in other ways. A compromise was finally reached when State Representative Eugene O'Flaherty proposed that both names be incorporated into the official title, the Leonard P. Zakim Bunker Hill Bridge.

Another rift that was never quite bridged pitted the chief engineer and architect, Christian Menn, against site managers and the engineer teams building the structure. Menn insisted, and tests later revealed, that a steel support beam was not properly reinforced with concrete. The problem was fixed, but not in the way he had recommended. Relations deteriorated to the point where Menn chose not to attend the ceremony dedicating his masterwork. However, the event did attract an impressive array of politicians and religious leaders as well as friends, family, and colleagues of Zakim, capped off by singer Bruce Springsteen's musical tribute to his friend. "This is a powerful teaching tool about this nation," Cardinal Bernard Law said of the structure afterwards. "It isn't just another bridge."

Financial District

Faneuil Hall

"If you don't know Funnel-Hall, you are no Boston boy," proclaims a character in James Fenimore Cooper's Revolutionary War novel *Lionel Lincoln*. Indeed, no building has historically been more identified with the city than Faneuil Hall, even if Bostonians could not always get their thick Yankee accents around its founder's French surname. "The last generation of schoolma'ms has taught us to call it 'Fan-you-well,' recalled historian Samuel Eliot Morison in 1921. If it took locals so long to get the name right, then visitors to the popular Freedom Trail site may be excused for still mispronouncing it.

Given Faneuil Hall's political and commercial significance to the community, it is surprising to learn that many Bostonians only reluctantly embraced the handsome brick building when it was completed in 1742. The wealthy French Huguenot merchant Peter Faneuil had offered it as a convenient place for country traders to market their goods, but many inhabitants preferred the custom of door-to-door vending.

Even with the support of Boston's first citizens and the addition of an upstairs meeting hall, Faneuil's generous gift was only narrowly accepted by a town vote. Yet no one opposed naming the building in his honor, and everyone was genuinely saddened by his sudden death just a few months later. Bostonians would mourn the loss of Faneuil Hall itself in 1761 when a fire gutted its interior, leaving them without their marketplace or meeting hall. They fortunately resolved to rebuild it, for Faneuil Hall was about to take its place at the center stage of history.

Faneuil Hall became famous as the "Cradle of Liberty" for its role in resisting British tyranny during the American Revolution. Upwards of a thousand people could gather inside to hear town meeting leaders such as Samuel Adams denounce the Stamp Act and other policies as threats to their constitutional rights as British citizens.

After Independence, Faneuil Hall became a favorite venue for political rallies, public banquets, and annual Fourth of July celebrations. Because of Faneuil Hall's popularity, the town hired architect Charles Bulfinch to expand the structure in 1805.

While tourist trinkets have supplemented foodstuffs in the marketplace and local government has gone elsewhere, Faneuil Hall still performs the same basic functions that it has since the eighteenth century—to provide a convenient place for the community to gather and exchange ideas as well as money. Unlike their ancestors, Bostonians today would not think of closing the market or reducing their meeting hall to a mere museum.

Previous page: Financial district skyline.

Custom House Tower

Often mistaken as Boston's first skyscraper, the 1915 Custom House Tower nonetheless does recall the age when the city began to grow up. Landfill projects enabled Boston to expand outward during the nineteenth century, but many businesses hesitated to leave lucrative, if confining, downtown locations. Real estate developers such as Frederick Lothrop Ames recognized the financial rewards of adding height to maximize commercial space, and in the early 1890s he hired George Shepley, Charles Coolidge, and Charles Rutan, former associates of the late H.H. Richardson, to design him the tallest building in Boston.

The emergence of steel-framed skyscrapers in the 1880s, most notably Chicago's ten-story Home Insurance Building, obviated the need for massive load-bearing walls and allowed Boston's buildings to reach new heights. The Custom House Tower was not the city's first structure to employ this new technology, an honor belonging to the Winthrop Building on Washington Street, but it did become the tallest after its completion in 1915. Architect Robert Peabody derived its design from the Campanile of St. Mark's in Venice. Buried beneath the new Italianate tower was the 1838 customhouse, a Greek Revival-style building that Walt Whitman once called "the noblest form of commercial architecture in the world." Located near some of the seaport's busiest wharves, it was at the heart of Boston's maritime trade. Nathaniel Hawthorne spent two mostly-miserable years as a measurer of salt and coal for the Boston Custom House while the new building was under construction. Hawthorne would probably find the Custom House a more hospitable environment today since Marriott Hotels renovated the building in 1997 for use as luxury suites.

Old City Hall

Even as the Civil War shook the nation's foundation in 1862, Bostonians were laying the foundation for a new City Hall on School Street. Now the Old City Hall, the building reflects the immense popularity of French Second Empire design in the late nineteenth century.

That a city hall was even deemed necessary speaks to the sea change of opinion regarding government in nineteenth-century Boston. Throughout the colonial era, residents had resisted calls for incorporation and the elimination of the town meeting system, which they considered more democratic. But by the early 1820s, many felt that the political process had become perverted, with local Federalist elites maintaining an iron grip on the town meeting. The financial hardships caused by the Panic of 1819 galvanized popular opposition to elite rule and created widespread support for incorporation. Leading the successful charge for change in 1822 was Josiah Quincy, a former Congressman who had had a falling-out with Federalist leaders.

Old City Hall served the community for a century, until the construction of Government Center in the late 1960s ended its days as the hub of local politics. Some of Boston's most famous mayors held reign there: Hugh O'Brien, the city's first Irish-born Catholic mayor; John F. Fitzgerald, maternal grandfather of President John F. Kennedy; James Michael Curley, "the people's mayor," who broke tradition by being inaugurated at spacious Tremont Temple rather than the confining City Hall; and John B. Hynes, who oversaw much of Boston's redevelopment in the 1950s. His successor, John Collins, was the last to serve in the building, abandoning it for the new modern-looking City Hall just before his term ended. Instead of facing the wrecking ball, however, Old City Hall was recycled for use as private office space, making it a pioneering example of adaptive reuse.

Big Dig

Two simple words describe the largest, most complex, and most expensive urban highway project in American history . . . Big Dig. Some speak of it proudly, amazed by the marvels of modern technology and human ingenuity. Others curse it under their breaths and shake their fists at the man most responsible for the costly project, the MIT-trained engineer Fred Salvucci.

While residents protested the freeway's impact on their neighborhoods, commuters sought alternate routes to avoid the congestion that increasingly manifested itself on the John F. Fitzgerald Expressway, as the Central Artery was officially known. By the year 2000, it was funneling upwards of 190,000 vehicles through Boston every day. The slightest fender-bender or smallest road obstruction could back up traffic for miles, defeating the freeway's purpose. As early as the 1970s, Salvucci had found a political ally in his efforts to bury the Expressway, Democratic state legislator Michael Dukakis. When Dukakis later became governor, he appointed Salvucci to be his Transportation Secretary.

Meanwhile, residents had become wary of such grand schemes after the Turnpike and Artery projects of the 1950s and 1960s. As late as 1989, Salvucci had yet to receive all the local building permits he needed to begin construction, and with every passing month the price tag rose by millions in interest.

The Big Dig finally broke ground in 1991 with construction of the Ted Williams Tunnel in South Boston, which would provide service to Logan Airport. Problems persisted even after parts of the Big Dig opened to motorists. In January of 2004 and again in September, water gushed through defective walls in the tunnel below South Station, tying up traffic for hours and adding to the project's incredible $14.6 billion price tag.

Old State House

"Then and there the child Independence was born," said John Adams of the Old State House, home to the colonial government. He was referring specifically to James Otis's 1761 defense of private property against general writs of assistance, which gave customs agents wide latitude to search for smuggled goods. "I will to my dying day," Otis declared, "oppose . . . all such instruments of slavery on the one hand, and villainy on the other, as this writ of assistance is." Although the Superior Court was unmoved, he won the hearts of Bostonians and was returned to the State House later that year as their representative to the legislature, where he became a thorn in the side of royal officials.

For much of the eighteenth century, the Old State House was better known as the New Town House, having replaced an earlier wooden structure after the Great Fire of 1711. Only after the town government moved to Faneuil Hall in the 1740s and the Beacon Hill State House was completed in 1797 did the noble brick building at the intersection of Washington and State Streets become "old." The site had originally been an open-air market where locals bought their provisions from country traders.

The State House was at the epicenter of the American Revolution in Boston. It was one of the few places where loyalists felt relatively safe from mob violence, especially after British troops set up headquarters on King Street and set up cannons before the State House doors in 1768. Their intimidating presence so offended James Otis that he requested government affairs be moved to Faneuil Hall. The powder keg that King Street had become exploded violently on the night of March 5, 1770, when British troops fired upon a taunting crowd, killing five civilians in the shadow of the State House.

Right: The Freedom Trail is a 3-mile walking tour of 16 sites and structures of historic importance in downtown Boston and Charlestown.

Old South Meetinghouse

The story of the Old South Meetinghouse is one of remarkable survival. Built in 1729, the "Sanctuary of Freedom," as it is often called, has withstood war, natural disasters, abandonment, and the often-destructive hand of progress to remind Bostonians of their glorious past. If the child Independence was born at the Old State House and nurtured at Faneuil Hall, then it was baptized at Old South Meetinghouse, where the Boston Tea Party is said to have originated. And long before he became a leading revolutionary, young Benjamin Franklin was also baptized at Old South in the days when its walls were still wooden. Indeed, baptism was even partly responsible for the church's founding in the seventeenth century.

Old South was born of a divisive theological dispute in the 1660s, the so-called "halfway covenant." Declining church membership threatened the future of religion in New England, because Puritans demanded that parents publicly profess their spiritual conversion before their children could be baptized. With fewer such professions taking place, however, some ministers argued that even the unconverted should be allowed to baptize their children under certain circumstances. But the Reverend John Davenport of Boston's First Church opposed such a reform, prompting some congregants to leave his ministry and found Old South in 1669.

City Hall Plaza

Decades after its construction, Boston City Hall and its extensive plaza are still as perplexing to casual tourists as they were to many locals when the plan was unveiled in 1962, one of whom purportedly asked, "What the hell is that?" Indeed, the much-maligned building has been variously described as a cement fortress, the crate that nearby Faneuil Hall came in, or just plain ugly. For residents used to the traditional styles of Charles Bulfinch and Asher Benjamin, City Hall seemed completely out of character for the city. Yet experts have praised its unusual design, which to some evokes ancient Mesoamerican architecture and to others exhibits the modern Brutalist style. The American Institute of Architects showered it with accolades and awards, and one of its chief designers, Gerhard Kallmann, remains convinced that Bostonians will eventually embrace the building.

Talk of relocating city officials from the beautiful, but cramped Old City Hall on School Street had been heard for years, though the idea floundered for lack of both funds and political will. The funds finally came in the form of federal urban renewal dollars, and the will was provided with the upset election of Mayor John Collins, who took office in 1960 promising a "New Boston." The new City Hall was to be the centerpiece of a much larger Government Center that would help revitalize the downtown district. Its location near Faneuil Hall, one of Boston's most venerated structures, presented unique challenges to the Columbia University architectural team chosen to design it.

Determined to give the building a contemporary look, yet sensitive to the history surrounding it, the architects decided on a style that emphasized horizontal rather than vertical lines.

Quincy Market

Boston's Quincy Market has become the envy of other American cities seeking to rehabilitate their commercial districts. Its wide array of shops, cafés, and special events create a festive atmosphere that attracts thousands of people to downtown Boston every year. On warm summer days, outdoor performers entertain crowds with everything from magic acts to dance routines, while inside the main market building vendors prepare smorgasbords of foods to please almost any palate. Whatever the season, the sights, sounds, and smells of Quincy Market can be quite intoxicating.

It was not always this way, however. Before the market was built in 1825, the area was a malodorous eyesore known as Town Cove. Generations of Bostonians had used it to dump their garbage, hoping the tide would take it out to sea. Instead, the cove became a stagnant pool of rotting food and broken wares from nearby Faneuil Hall marketplace. It also acted as an unceremonious final resting place for dead pets.

Stiff ocean winds and warm temperatures carried the stench into surrounding streets, prompting public health concerns as well as embarrassing the community. "In the season of danger the sons of fortune can seek refuge in purer atmospheres," noted Josiah Quincy. "But necessity condemns the poor to remain and inhale the noxious effluvia [vapors]."

Quincy Market lost much of its allure in the early twentieth century when businesses plastered their signs and billboards all over its once-beautiful façade, now blackened from decades of accumulated soot. Suburban growth in the post-World War II era pulled people out of the market toward the shiny new malls and supermarkets in surrounding towns. Both the building and its business had deteriorated so much that there was serious talk about tearing it

down in the 1950s. Naysayers argued that Quincy Market's best days were behind it, that it could never again be a vibrant commercial center.

Exactly who is responsible for resuscitating the dying the market is unclear. Some credit historian Walter Muir Whitehill's campaign to raise public awareness of Quincy Market's historical significance. Others point to Edward J. Logue, director of the Boston Redevelopment Authority in the 1960s, or to Mayor Kevin White, who championed urban renewal. Still others praise the vision and persistence of Benjamin and Jane Thompson, architects of the festival marketplace idea that has animated Quincy Market since its 1976 rededication. All likely deserve some measure of credit for what is widely considered Boston's best urban renewal effort and a model for others to follow.

Financial District

Boston's financial district blossomed in the nineteenth century, but its roots can be found in the colonial period. Since the late seventeenth century, leading merchants had gathered around the Old State House to discuss market conditions at home and abroad. Many lived in the surrounding streets; their fine homes intermingled with shops and storehouses near the waterfront. However, the development of new residential neighborhoods drew them away from State Street after the Revolution, giving the area a predominately commercial character.

Unfortunately, the area bore the brunt of devastation during the Great Fire of 1872, which leveled nearly forty acres and bankrupted scores of companies. A thriving new business district emerged out of the ashes of the old after 1872. In 1891, the Boston Stock Exchange moved into its new home at 53 State Street, a twelve-story granite structure capable of housing over a thousand offices. Nearly a century later, the building was attached to a forty-story glass skyscraper to form the Exchange Place office complex.

Federal deregulation of the banking and finance industries along with a robust local economy, dubbed the "Massachusetts Miracle," reinvigorated Boston's financial district in the 1980s, resulting in new construction such as Exchange Place. Built at a cost of $97 million in 1985, Exchange Place helped reverse decades of decline in Boston's financial district. Once considered a "9 to 5 neighborhood," the area has also recently become home to several trendy nightclubs and restaurants, dispelling the notion that the financial district is all work and no play.

View of financial district from Quincy Market.

The Province House Steps

A set of granite garden stairs are all that is left to mark the site of the Province House, which was the royal governor's mansion in the eighteenth century. Originally built in 1679 for the wealthy merchant Peter Sergeant, the home ranked among Boston's finest for its distinctive Dutch architectural design. Sergeant had lived there nearly twenty years before a change in government created the need for a stately mansion to serve the royal governor. In 1698, he agreed to rent the home to the newly arrived governor, Richard Coote, Earl of Bellomont. Sergeant's death in 1714 enabled provincial officials to purchase the sizeable property, including its various outbuildings and formal gardens, for an official governor's residence.

During the Revolution, the once elegant mansion began to assume the appearance of an abandoned house, as the rebelling legislature slashed its funding. Governor Thomas Hutchinson was shocked by its dilapidated condition and embarrassed to live there. "It is a dishonour to His Majesty's Commission that the Governor lives in it in its present state," he griped to London officials. The residence was also heavily guarded by British soldiers and eventually became the headquarters for Generals Gage and Howe during the siege of Boston. In 1851, the interior was gutted and remodeled for use as a minstrel theater, and it was finally torn down in 1922.

New England Holocaust Memorial

Erected along the Freedom Trail in 1995, the New England Holocaust Memorial is perhaps the most moving piece of public art in the city. Six luminous glass towers reach toward the heavens, carrying with them numbers representing each of the Holocaust's six million Jewish victims. Below are metal grates covering smoking pits that recall the Nazis' six principal death camps. A black granite path leads visitors through the solemn towers and past inscriptions from those who bore witness to the tragedy. Gypsies, homosexuals, and other persecuted groups are remembered alongside the Jews who bore the brunt of suffering.

Chosen from over 500 designs, Stanley Saitowitz's complex memorial is as emotional as it is educational, and it has drawn favorable comparisons to Maya Lin's Vietnam Veterans Memorial in Washington, D.C. Both express unspeakable sadness in terms that enable the observer to find personal meaning in their abstract forms. "There are many different ways to interpret it," says Saitowitz of the memorial. "The towers can be seen as the smokestacks from the death chambers. At night when they are lit, they will be almost like candles to the remembrance of the dead."

Jewish Holocaust survivors living in New England were the driving force behind the memorial, though funds for the $3.5 million project came from a variety of public and private sources. Jews had begun coming to Boston in large numbers toward the end of the nineteenth century, many fleeing persecution in Eastern Europe. They initially joined other immigrant groups in the crowded North End before venturing elsewhere in the city as circumstances allowed.

Chinatown

There may be no better example of Boston's evolution as a city than Chinatown. Once nothing more than a barren mudflat, it has become the densest residential neighborhood in the city and the heart of the city's Asian-American community. Over the course of the colonial era, a number of wharves and shipyards were built along what was then known as South Cove, but substantial commercial and residential development did not begin until the nineteenth century. Landfill projects gradually shrunk the cove into a mere channel by the 1840s and paved the way for a fashionable new South Boston neighborhood.

However, South Boston quickly fell out of fashion with the subsequent development of Back Bay, as well as the influx of Irish laborers working in its rail yards and living in the neighborhood's growing number of tenements. The rail lines also brought Chinese immigrants in the 1870s, mostly men who may have worked on the recently completed Transcontinental Railroad. Although they were few in number and settled in obscure side streets such as Oliver Place (now Ping On

Alley) and Oxford Place, they nonetheless excited the prejudices of others and quickened the exodus from the neighborhood. Irish laborers, fearing new job competition, joined with nativists in calling for restrictions on Chinese immigration, which resulted in the Chinese Exclusion Act of 1882. The newcomers also faced harassment from local police, who in 1903 arrested hundreds of Chinatown residents and deported nearly fifty under the pretext of public safety. Most of the Chinese immigrants scraped by working in laundries and restaurants such as Hong Far Low, founded in 1879 on Harrison Avenue.

The most famous of Chinatown's restaurants, however, was Ruby Foo's Den on Hudson Street. Opened in 1929, its renowned cuisine and exotic architecture attracted all sorts of Bostonians who otherwise might never have visited the neighborhood. Ruby Foo's success spawned a number of imitators, and by the 1950s many establishments were catering to non-Chinese customers by Americanizing their names and altering their menus. Yet the community never lost touch with its heritage.

Theater District

One wonders what the old Puritans would think of Boston's theater district, centered on Boylston, Tremont, and Stuart Streets south of the Common. Their religious scruples made them suspicious of actors and their credulous audiences, who made tempting targets for the wily Satan. When the Reverend Increase Mather learned of a local tavernkeeper's efforts to stage shows, he denounced the scheme as a "danger to the souls of Men." Such self-righteous attitudes gained the force of law in 1750, making it a crime to sponsor, perform, or even attend plays. Theatergoers were driven underground, fearing less the wrath of God than the fury of their neighbors. After authorities raided the makeshift Board Alley Theater in 1792, a gang of toughs threatened to tear it down.

None would have dared destroy the elegant new playhouse that Charles Bulfinch designed for the community just two years later. The Federal Street Theater, as it was best known, indicated a growing acceptance of the stage as the mark of a civilized people rather than heathens. Its patrons were drawn primarily from the ranks of the city's merchant elite, while artisans and mechanics preferred the rival Haymarket Theater. Built near the corner of Boylston and Tremont Streets in 1796, the Haymarket was the first theater to inhabit the modern Theater District. It proved a poor precedent, however, for it lasted less than a decade and failed to attract other playhouses to the area.

Before the Civil War, theaters tended to be concentrated downtown at the other end of Tremont Street, northeast of the Common, where most Bostonians lived and worked. An important exception was the Boston Theater in the South End, opened on Washington Street in 1854. With seating for 3,000, it was billed as "the largest and most magnificent theatre in America" and also served as an opera house. A cluster of playhouses emerged around the Boston Theater in the 1860s and 1870s, creating the first traces of a theater district. Among them was the 1879 Park Theater. Today the old Park Theater is the lone playhouse left standing from nineteenth-century Boston. As for the Boston Theater, only its foundation survives as part of the Opera House.

The Waterfront

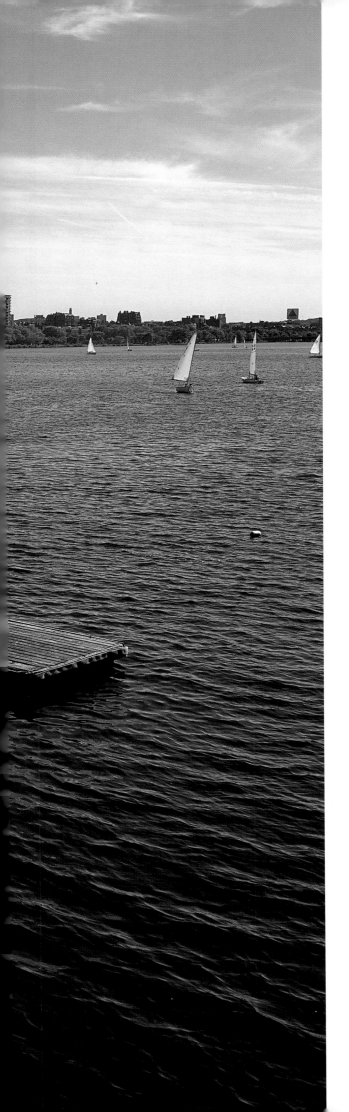

Community Boating

O f the many ways to take in the sights and sounds of Boston, few are more satisfying than a sail along the Charles River courtesy of Community Boating. Joseph Lee, Jr. founded Community Boating back in 1936 to provide Depression-era youths with a unique outlet for their energies and a chance to enjoy nature. At that time, the Charles River was beginning to come into its own as a recreational site. Construction of the Charles River Dam in 1910 blocked the harbor tides that had once made it a muddy mess, transforming it into a more navigable fresh-water river. The Esplanade quickly followed and in the 1930s was redesigned through the philanthropy of Helen Osbourne Storrow. Among the improvements made at this time were the addition of boat landings and the creation of Storrow Lagoon for summer sailing and winter skating. Storrow's money also furnished the increasingly popular Community Boating with a new boathouse in 1941.

The hallmark of Community Boating has always been its work with children and young adults. Boston University's sailing team practiced there in the 1950s before acquiring its own facility. By that time, Community Boating maintained a fleet of thirty fiberglass Mercury boats for kids to enjoy through its Junior Program. Even today, boys and girls can join for only one dollar and participate in all kinds of activities, including the annual "Kids Sail the Stars" regatta that lets them race with some of the sport's best athletes. A number of area high school sailing programs also owe their existence to support from Community Boating, which provides equipment otherwise beyond the reach of many school districts.

Because Community Boating is a non-profit organization, it relies on modest membership fees from adults to maintain its youth programs. Fortunately, grown-ups are as anxious to climb aboard as the kids. The stalwarts arrive early on Opening Day, April 1, and are often among the last off the boats when the season ends on Halloween. In between, thousands of casual members from all walks of life come to relax on the docks, attend barbeque picnics, and take romantic midnight sails. Such activities have helped make Community Boating the largest organization of its kind in the United States, and its contributions to both the sailing world and the community of Boston have earned it countless awards.

Pages 100–101: Lewis Wharf.

Custom House Block

Built around 1837, the granite-faced Custom House Block on Boston's Long Wharf reflects an era when the seaport was alive with maritime activity. Architect Isaiah Rogers, who had recently completed work on nearby Commercial Wharf, designed the four-story warehouse building to replace several smaller wooden warehouses that had sat on the wharf since the colonial period. Walking along Boston's waterfront in the 1840s, Alexander Mackay was amazed by the abundance that characterized the Custom House Block. "[T]hickly strewn around you, are all the insignia of an extensive commerce," he wrote. "Raw cotton in countless bales; piles of manufactured goods for the South American and Chinese markets; whole acres covered with parallel rows of clean white barrels, some of them well-nigh busting with flour, others full of salt."

Although the decline of Boston's waterfront in the twentieth century rendered the Custom House Block obsolete as a warehouse, the federal government recognized the structure's importance to maritime history by naming it a National Historic Landmark in 1966, which protected it from demolition. It thereafter became an important part of the city's renewal plan for the waterfront district. In the early 1970s, Anderson Notter Associates, the architectural firm that won praise for its renovation of Boston's Old City Hall, adapted the Custom House Block for reuse as office and living space.

Long Wharf Marina

If Boston is the "hub" of the universe, as Oliver Wendell Holmes once suggested, then Long Wharf is historically the hub of Boston. Built between 1710 and 1713, it extended an unprecedented 800 feet into Boston Harbor, enabling large vessels to unload their cargo directly onto the dock. Wooden warehouses lined the north side of the wharf, and upwards of 50 ships could moor there at any given time. Located at the foot of King (now State) Street, it both reflected and contributed to Boston's commercial growth in the eighteenth century. Some of the best inns and coffeehouses in the city could be found there, patronized by everyone from customs agents to merchant smugglers.

Today, Long Wharf has almost wholly been given over to recreation. New forms of shipping reduced the commercial need for the wharf, contributing to decades of decline before the urban renewal initiatives of the 1960s. While hotels have replaced the old warehouses than once lined the wharf, passenger ferries occupy the moorings formerly reserved for merchant vessels. And the Waterboat Marina allows for more pleasure boats to enjoy the wharf, although it has become a source of controversy in recent years. Critics complain that its tax rate has not kept pace with rising property values along the wharf, but officials insist that the marina's role in attracting wealth to the waterfront is worth more than the added tax dollars that might drive it under.

Chart House

For a taste of Old Boston, few restaurants can match the Chart House. Its waterfront location and historic setting not only offer ambiance, but also provide lessons in the past. The four-story Gardner Building that houses the restaurant was originally a warehouse, one of many that once lined the harbor. Most experts agree that it was constructed sometime in the 1760s and used by John Hancock, although at least one scholar dates it to the 1830s. In either case, it is the oldest building of its kind on the waterfront. Centuries of wear and tear had left it in a ramshackle condition when the Colorado-based Chart House purchased it.

Since its founding in 1961, the Chart House has a long tradition of restoring historic structures for its restaurants, especially those with ties to America's maritime heritage. Work on the Gardner Building included bracing its brick walls, redesigning the first floor for a dining room, and adding kitchen space. Despite the remodeling and a damaging 1997 fire, the structure still possesses original elements and is decorated with items evoking Boston's colonial days. The restaurant's menu features such local favorites as New England clam chowder as well as more exotic items such as Chilean Sea Bass. The Chart House's success in Boston and elsewhere prompted its sale to Landry's Restaurants in 2002, making it part of the nation's second leading seafood chain.

New England Aquarium

Sea lions and tiger sharks and barracudas, oh my! For an undersea adventure unlike any other, follow the road to the New England Aquarium on Boston's Central Wharf. Since its opening in 1969, the Aquarium has educated and entertained boatloads of visitors with its giant, 200,000-gallon ocean tank, one of the largest in the world. Swimming inside the four-story tank, which features a replica coral reef, are a wide variety of tropical fish and other marine life, including moray eels and several sharks. Myrtle the Sea Turtle has been the tank's star attraction

Above: Fish and diver.

for over thirty-five years, during which time she has seen the Aquarium grow up around her. Indeed, it has evolved from a rather simple box-like building into an elaborate complex that has helped revitalize Boston's waterfront.

The Aquarium's staff is committed to educating the public about the challenges that sea-creatures face in the changing global environment of the twenty-first century. To that end, they maintain a research facility where scholars are currently studying a disease that affects shellfish and threatens fisheries. There is also a library and a teachers' resource center for educators to find useful classroom material. For more hands-on learning, students can take Boston Harbor boat trips that teach them basic research techniques. The Aquarium often lends its expertise and facilities to help rescue and care for stranded or injured marine animals.

Right: Penguins.

Rowes Wharf

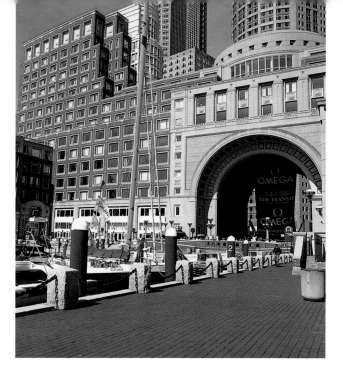

With its luxury hotel suites and majestic harbor views, Rowes Wharf is the crowning achievement of a decades-long effort to redevelop Boston's historic waterfront district, which had deteriorated badly in the twentieth century. In marked contrast to its current commercial and recreational character, the site began as a military installation designed to defend against French naval assaults in the colonial era. By the time of the American Revolution, it also included the wharf and warehouses of merchant John Rowe, for whom the area is still named.

But for his wharf, Bostonians might no longer remember John Rowe. Royal officials could hardly forget him, however. They branded him a rebel for his involvement in the patriot movement, and Rowe endured repeated harassment at the hands of British troops as a result.

The end of the war and the return of trade revived Boston's waterfront, with ships bound for ports all over the world leaving from Rowes Wharf. Packet boats brought growing numbers of Irish immigrants to the seaport by the 1840s, many of whom lived in crowded Fort Hill tenements near Rowes Wharf. Rail service to and from the pier kept it bustling, as did the Nantasket Beach steamers that ferried Bostonians to the popular Paragon Park amusement park in the early twentieth century.

The Great Depression and the advent of new forms of transportation slowed activity at Rowes Wharf, which by mid-century functioned mostly as a parking lot for nearby shops and businesses. It was indicative of just how much the city had turned away from its maritime traditions. Rowes Wharf did not receive the same attention as other urban renewal projects of the 1950s and 1960s, but in the 1980s it caught the eye of the Beacon Companies, a real estate development firm that recognized its commercial potential.

The Beacon Companies hired Chicago architect Adrian Smith to redesign Rowes Wharf, which was to feature luxury condominiums, hotel rooms, restaurants, and office space as well as a marina and ferryboat launch. After decades of decline, Rowes Wharf is again a vital part of the Boston waterfront.

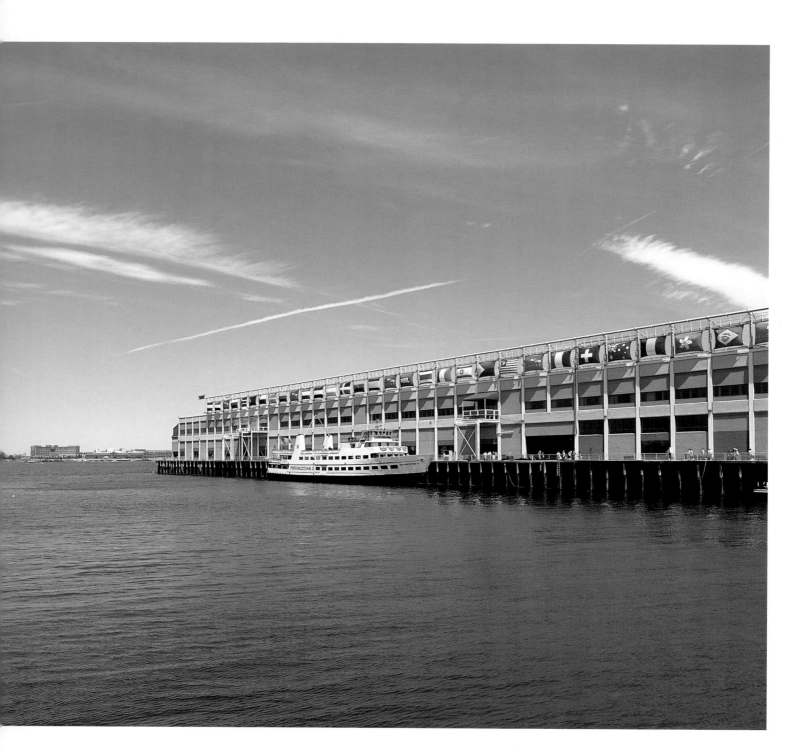

Ferries to Provincetown

Savvy travelers know that the best way to bypass the summer traffic jams out on Cape Cod is by boat. Besides, no car ride can compare with the scenic views offered aboard the ferries that connect Boston's Long Wharf and World Trade Center piers to historic Provincetown, where the *Mayflower* Pilgrims landed before moving on to Plymouth in 1620. A 252-foot high tower commemorates their brief stay and provides a breathtaking panorama of the Cape. Provincetown's natural beauty may not have been enough to keep the Pilgrims, but it has attracted writers, artists, and poets for over a century, including such notables as Jackson Pollock and Norman Mailer. It remains a magnet for those seeking an alternative lifestyle.

Boston Children's Museum

Founded in 1913, the Boston Children's Museum is the legacy of progressive-minded teachers who believed that active learning was a "hands-on" experience, not a trait typically associated with museums. This innovative approach to education had been pioneered by the Brooklyn Children's Museum in 1899, making the Boston museum just the second institution of its kind in the country. Its early collection reflected the scientific interests of its founders, with activities that sought to reconnect city kids with the wonders of the natural world. It continues this tradition with such exhibits as the Science Playground. More recently, however, the museum has come to emphasize the arts and humanities.

By 1979, the museum had outgrown its original Jamaica Plains home and moved into an old woolens warehouse along Fort Point Channel, where it remains today.

Many of the museum's exhibits and programs aim to teach children the value of cultural diversity. In 2005, the Children's Museum announced plans for a major renovation and expansion that will add 20,000 square feet of space to the

Recycle exhibit.

existing facility. Improvements will emphasize exhibits that promote healthful, active lifestyles in children, an issue of growing concern in contemporary American society. Proper nutrition has been a theme of the museum ever since its affiliation with a forty-foot milk bottle began back in the 1970s. Built in the 1930s for a homemade ice-cream shop, the whimsical wooden carving was later purchased by the Hood Company, New England's largest dairy, and moved to Museum Wharf, where it functions as a refreshment stand.

Fenway

Museum of Fine Arts

These are exciting times for Boston's Museum of Fine Arts. Already one of America's largest and most prestigious cultural institutions, the museum launched an unprecedented $425 million expansion and renovation in 2002 that will transform its Huntington Avenue home before the end of the decade. Director Malcolm Rogers has led the MFA out of debt by tapping new revenue streams and sponsoring innovative exhibitions that have pushed annual attendance past the million mark. Much of the museum's massive collection is also being digitized for viewing on the worldwide web, and leading art experts such as Christraud Geary, MFA's first curator of African art, have been attracted to the dynamic institution.

The origins of the Museum of Fine Arts extend back two centuries to the 1807 founding of the Boston Athenaeum, which patronized the arts as well as literature. Over the decades, its growing collection of portraits and sculptures began to outstrip the Beacon Hill building's ability to contain it. A proposed donation of medieval armor in 1869 sent Athenaeum officials scurrying to the state legislature for approval to create a fine arts museum. The trustees of the new museum, many of whom were affiliated with the Athenaeum and swanky social clubs such as St. Botolph, were granted land along Copley Square for a Gothic revival building designed by John Sturgis and Charles Brigham. (Ironically, the armor collection never made it into the museum, having been destroyed in the Great Fire of 1872.)

The new museum, one of the first of its kind in the United States, proved an instant success when it opened on July 4, 1876. Over 150,000 people visited it in its first year of operation, and private donations of art and money began pouring in. To this day, the MFA is almost entirely funded through private means. Despite two additions to the building, however, it was bursting at the seams by 1899 and abandoned for

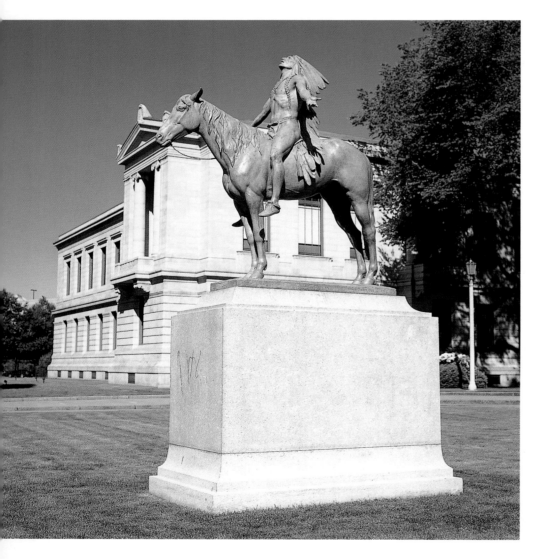

Previous page: Charles River Basin.

Left: At the entrance to the museum is Cyrus Dallin's Native American statue Appeal to the Great Spirit, completed in 1909. Dalin also sculpted the historic statue Paul Revere, which is near the Old North Church.

Tenshin-En, a 10,000-square-foot Japanese rock garden. Named in honor of Okakura Tenshin, an esteemed former curator of the museum's vast Asiatic art collection, Tenshin-En means "Garden of the Heart of Heaven." This contemplative space was created in the kare-sansui style, drawing on a combination of elements from Japan as well as New England, reinterpreting the ancient art form of the Zen temple gardens of 15th-century Japan.

the museum's current location, near Frederick Law Olmsted's Emerald Necklace park system. Architect Guy Lowell provided the MFA's now-familiar neoclassical façade in 1909, while Cyrus Dallin designed the eye-catching sculpture *An Appeal to the Great Spirit* that greets visitors outside the Huntington Street entrance. Erected in 1913, the statue captures the contemporary concern over a supposedly vanishing American frontier as well as reflecting the museum's interest in indigenous art and culture.

Most of the MFA's early collection featured European and Euro-American artwork, including portraits by Gilbert Stuart and some of Paul Revere's silver. It proudly possesses one of the largest collections of Claude Monet's paintings found outside of Paris. But the museum has also developed outstanding non-Western and Ancient World collections. Visitors are sometimes surprised to find themselves surrounded by Egyptian mummies and samurai swords in the middle of Boston. Indeed, the MFA's collections

encompass far more than the predictable paintings and portraits; they feature everything from unusual musical instruments and textiles to rare Roman coins.

The museum's recent renaissance has not been without controversy, however. Curators who questioned its direction were dismissed, while the director has come under fire for certain fundraising tactics. In 2004, valuable Monet paintings were loaned to the Bellagio Casino's unaccredited art gallery, a deal that generated a million dollars for the MFA. But critics argued that the risk to the artwork was too great, especially after a power outage temporarily left the Las Vegas gallery without climate-control. Others accused the non-profit museum of abusing its tax-exempt status with such "fast buck" schemes. Undaunted, Malcolm Rogers remains committed to making the "new" Museum of Fine Arts, in his words, "a landmark in our community and a magnet for visitors who come to Boston."

Massachusetts Historical Society

Founded by Reverend Jeremy Belknap in 1791, the Massachusetts Historical Society was the first organization of its kind in the country and remains one of the nation's most prestigious historical societies. Belknap had been a staunch supporter of the American Revolution who believed that history was the way to knit the new United States together. Yet he was also aware that this would prove impossible without the creation of a repository for researchers to find the necessary documents, a problem that he had encountered while working on a history of New Hampshire.

Belknap initially approached Harvard College with his idea, but decided to found an independent historical society after school officials dragged their feet on the matter. Membership was originally limited to thirty, all of whom had to be serious about helping the society prosper. Belknap personally donated his extensive collection of books and manuscripts to get the archive started and solicited dona-

tions from others as the corresponding secretary of the Society.

The Massachusetts Historical Society relocated to its current home at 1154 Boylston Street in 1899. The new headquarters exuded an air of culture and sophistication, though it proved somewhat impractical as a research facility.

The Society nearly closed its doors in 1950 due to decades of mounting debt caused by war and economic depression. Officials swallowed their pride and asked the public for aid to pull the organization back from the brink of bankruptcy. It worked. By the end of the decade, the Society was again thriving and even considered admitting women members into its all-male ranks. It would take several years to wear down resistance to the idea, but in the late 1960s the first female scholars were finally invited to join.

Today the Massachusetts Historical Society attracts scholars from all over the world, drawn to Boylston Street by the organization's rich archives and extensive fellowship program.

Isabella Stewart Gardner Museum

"Unique." "Eclectic." "Innovative." "Enchanting." These words and more have been used to describe the Isabella Stewart Gardner Museum, home to some of the world's most valuable works of art. One would hardly know it looking at the museum's unassuming exterior, however. In contrast to the classical columns and colossal size of other museums, Gardner's collection is housed in a fifteenth-century Venetian palazzo that reflects its founder's fascination with the Italian Renaissance. Guests often assume that it was once a private residence, but in fact Mrs. Gardner expressly built it as an art museum after her husband's sudden death in 1898.

Isabella Stewart Gardner was something of a mystery to Bostonians. Born in New York of Scottish descent, she was a child of privilege with a strong sense of *noblesse oblige*. Her father made a fortune in various nineteenth-century industries and sent the teenaged Isabella to school in Paris, where she began a lifelong love affair with European culture. Her marriage to John Lowell Gardner, Jr., son of a wealthy merchant-industrialist, brought her to Boston's Beacon Hill in the 1860s. "Mrs. Jack," as Isabella was known in polite circles, endured the loss of her only child in 1865 and a subsequent malaise that only extensive European travel remedied. Convinced that America lacked art and culture, she made it her mission to fill that void with her museum and befriended others who shared her passion, including the painter John Singer Sargent, novelist Henry James, and art critic Bernard Berenson among others.

But Gardner became as famous around Boston for her personal eccentricities as for her art collection. She supposedly drank beer while other ladies sipped tea. Many of these stories are greatly exaggerated, yet at least one is known to be true. After her beloved Red Sox won the 1912 World Series, she shocked proper society by attending the Boston Symphony wearing a conspicuous headband reading "Oh, you Red Sox!" The stunt may have offended concertgoers, but endeared her to the hearts of generations of Red Sox fans, who can receive a discount on museum admission by sporting team paraphernalia.

Narrow hallways, cozy alcoves, and antique furnishings create an intimacy that enhances its aesthetics. And few can resist visiting the central courtyard, with its fragrant flowers cultivated in the museum's own greenhouses. It is indeed easy to lose oneself in the experience, wandering amidst the thousands of paintings, sculptures, tapestries, and ceramics that comprise the collection.

Marsh Chapel

Since its dedication in 1950, Marsh Chapel has served as both the architectural and spiritual center of the Boston University campus. Its name has nothing to do with the marshlands, or fens, that once dominated the area. Rather, the building is named in honor of Daniel L. Marsh, the school's long-time president, who was instrumental in its creation. "Let this chapel at the center of the university campus," wrote Marsh, in words now inscribed above the chapel door, "signify forever the centrality both of intellectual and experimental religion in education and also of devotion to God's righteous rule in human lives."

The end of World War II and the opening of Marsh Chapel began a new chapter in Boston University's history. The Methodist school had spent decades wandering from Brookline to Beacon Hill to Copley Square before settling along the Charles River in the 1920s. But war and depression hampered its growth and shifted its priorities. Over two hundred students and alumni died serving their country in World War II, including the Reverend George L. Fox. Fox was one of four army chaplains who sacrificed their lifejackets and their lives to save others aboard the sinking U.S.S. *Dorchester* in February of 1943.

In later years a young man from Atlanta, Georgia, named Martin Luther, King, Jr., began doctoral coursework at Boston University's renowned School of Theology. He came contemplating a career in academia, but graduated in 1955 determined to be a preacher after falling under the spell of Howard Thurman, the first black dean of Marsh Chapel. Thurman's message of Christian tolerance and compassion touched the hearts of his diverse congregation, which crowded into the chapel to hear his sermons.

Open to people of all faiths, Marsh Chapel and its adjoining plaza have provided students with a place to come together in celebration, protest, and mourning.

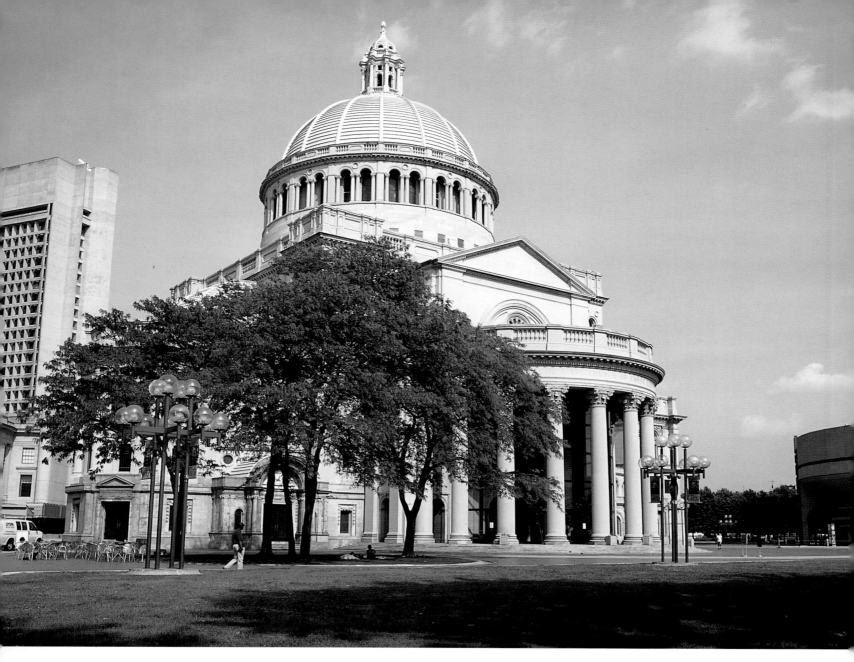

The (Christian Science) Mother Church

Puritanism has cast such a long shadow over Boston's religious history that the city's role in other prominent religious movements is often overlooked. Yet it is hard to miss the century-old Mother Church that has served as headquarters for the First Church of Christ, Scientist for over a century. The sprawling fourteen-acre complex, complete with a reflecting pool, water fountain, and an unusual three-story glass globe (called the Mapparium), attracts some 250,000 visitors a year, even as church membership declines and financial difficulties mount. Critics argue that Christian Science itself has become like the 1935 Mapparium, a hollow shell frozen in time, but believers are banking on the country's recent

conservative turn and renewed emphasis on faith to help restore the church to its former glory.

A recent $60 million renovation of the Mother Church along with the opening of the visitor center and library suggest that church leaders remain optimistic about the future. There are other hopeful signs as well. In 2002, the *Christian Science Monitor* won its seventh Pulitzer Prize. Plans are also in the works to restore Eddy's Victorian mansion in Chestnut Hill, where she spent the last three years of her life establishing the *Monitor*. And the Library continues to sponsor popular community events aimed at encouraging youths to creatively express themselves.

Muddy River

As its name suggests, Muddy River is a rather murky stream that empties into the Charles River and forms the boundary between Boston and Brookline to the west. In the colonial period, its fertile banks were prized farmland for some of Puritan Boston's leading citizens, including Reverend John Cotton and Judge Samuel Sewall. A small agricultural settlement emerged there by the early eighteenth century, and Muddy River farmers were among those who carted their produce through the streets of Boston to Faneuil Hall market.

The river would likely be of little note today were it not for Frederick Law Olmsted's efforts to feature it in his famed Emerald Necklace park system. Not everyone shared his enthusiasm for the project, however. Brookline had been fighting off annexation by Boston since the 1870s and was reluctant to sell its share of the Muddy River, delaying the development of Riverway Park until the 1890s. Olmsted's improvements, which better controlled silt deposits, made Muddy River something of a misnomer and transformed an otherwise nondescript stream into a popular recreational retreat. Recent pollution problems have again muddied its waters and tarnished Olmsted's Emerald Necklace, prompting public campaigns to clean up Muddy River as both an historic and natural treasure for the community.

Fenway Park

Fenway Park, home of the Boston Red Sox, is a Mecca for baseball fans worldwide. Every year, millions of them make a pilgrimage and pay homage to this "Cathedral of Baseball," the oldest stadium in the major leagues. They come to connect with the sport's storied past, watch current stars play ball, and perhaps catch a glimpse of a future Hall-of-Famer. For many fans, Fenway Park is also an indelible part of their personal history, a magical place their parents took them as kids or where they spent a memorable afternoon with their own children. And players likewise never forget the first time they stepped onto the legendary field where some of the game's greatest athletes have performed. Perhaps former pitcher Tom Seaver put it best when he said, "Fenway is the essence of baseball."

Before the construction of Fenway Park in 1912, the Red Sox leased a stadium on Huntington Avenue, where the first World Series was played in 1903. But owner John I. Taylor found the arrangement unacceptable and determined to build a new facility on land being developed by his real estate company, a move that enhanced the value of both the land and the team. He called the structure Fenway Park because of its location. The team's home opener, played in the wake of the *Titanic* tragedy, drew nearly 27,000 spectators and began a banner year for the Red Sox, who went on to win the 1912 World Series. Two years later Babe Ruth started his brilliant career as a Sox pitcher before being sold to the New York Yankees in 1920.

And so began the infamous "Curse of the Bambino." Ruth's departure ended a decade of dominance and initiated a steady decline that saw the club struggle both on and off the field. There was even talk of closing Fenway Park. An organization that was repeatedly crowned champions in the 1910s could no longer even post a winning record and would not win the World Series for the rest of the century! Meanwhile,

Ruth's Yankees opened their new stadium in 1923 with a victory over the Red Sox and went on to win the first of their record twenty-six World Series titles.

Things began to look up for the Fenway faithful when millionaire Thomas A. Yawkey purchased the Red Sox in 1933. Several years later in 1939, he brought in "The Kid," Ted Williams, to play in front of the monstrous wall. Williams would become a fixture in left field for the next twenty years, although most of his 521 career home runs went over the right field fence, an area nicknamed "Williamsburg."

Any lingering uncertainty about the team's future at Fenway was effectively buried along with "the Curse" in 2004, when the Red Sox won their first World Series since 1918.

Frederick Law Olmsted National Historic Park

Although Frederick Law Olmsted is best known as the architect of New York City's Central Park, the native New Englander spent much of his distinguished career in suburban Boston, where he designed a series of interconnected parks affectionately called the "Emerald Necklace." Olmsted was brought to Boston in 1878, at the behest of public officials concerned about the city's stifling effects on its residents. Boston Common, long a retreat from the hustle and bustle of urban life, seemed smaller with each passing year as the city expanded around it.

Olmsted's plan called for the Common, the Public Garden, and the recently completed Commonwealth Avenue Mall to be joined with new parks beginning at Charlesgate, near where the Muddy River meets the Charles River, and continuing south through the Back Bay Fens and Jamaica Pond before finishing at Franklin Park, the crown jewel of the necklace. Columbia Road was to have been the next link in the chain, but was never completed after Olmsted's death in 1903.

Perhaps to better supervise his ambitious

project, Olmsted left Manhattan in 1883 for a Brookline farmhouse near the Emerald Necklace and close to his friend H.H. Richardson, architect of Boston's Trinity Church. The 1810 home also doubled as an office until construction of a formal office complex on the property began in 1889. An old hay barn was refurbished to provide additional office space for Olmsted and his sons Frederick, Jr. and John Charles, who assisted their father with his expanding business. As one would expect from America's premiere landscape architect, his 1.76-acre estate, which he named "Fairsted," was beautifully designed and featured elements also applied to the Emerald Necklace. Although many original plants and trees have naturally succumbed to the ravages of time, the grounds remain much as they

appeared in Olmsted's day, including the 150-year-old "Olmsted Elm."

After declining health forced Olmsted into retirement in 1895, his sons capably maintained both the firm and the farm well into the twentieth century. Frederick, Jr. helped create the National Park Service, which ironically would assume ownership of Fairsted and its rich archival collection in 1979. A major, two-year renovation of the site began in 2005 to improve fire protection, remodel the barn for public use, and address drainage problems on the property. Were he alive, Frederick Law Olmsted might have some expert advice on that last matter, for proper drainage was the key to building his Emerald Necklace along the marshy lowlands of Boston's Back Bay.

John F. Kennedy National Historic Site

Casually passing by the humble, two-and-a-half story home at 83 Beals Street in Brookline, one might not realize that it was the birthplace of President John Fitzgerald Kennedy. John's parents, Joseph and Rose, purchased the house shortly after their marriage in 1914, when Brookline was a fashionable address for many wealthy Bostonians. Joseph had just begun a career as a banker and investor, while Rose was the well-known daughter of former Boston mayor John F. Fitzgerald, for whom the future President was named.

Rose Fitzgerald Kennedy fondly recalled their years in the home, saying "We were very happy here and although we did not know about the days ahead, we were enthusiastic and optimistic about the future." But she and her husband endured plenty of trials and tribulations there as well. Beginning with the birth of Joseph Jr. in 1915, Rose was nearly always either pregnant or nursing. Baby pictures of the four children born in the house are on display today, as is the bed where John Kennedy was born in 1917. He proved to be a rather sickly child, battling everything from measles, mumps, and whooping cough to a serious bout of scarlet fever that sent him to the hospital in 1920. His worried father was a near constant companion at his bedside, and Rose would spend time at home reading books to young John in the nursery.

By 1921, the house on Beals Street was becoming crowded and Joseph's financial success enabled them to move into a large Victorian home on nearby Naples Street. A few years later, they left Brookline altogether. The family and the town rediscovered the house after John Kennedy was elected president, affixing an historical plaque to its exterior in 1961. Kennedy's assassination two years later prompted his mother to repurchase the home, furnish it with family heirlooms, and donate it to the federal government for preservation as a national historic landmark. She even recorded an audio house tour for visitors to the site. "It is our intention and hope to make a gift of this home to the American people so that future generations will be able to visit it and see how people lived in 1917 and thus get a better appreciation of the history of this wonderful country," she explained.

Right: Television studio where reporter Walter Cronkite covered the 1960 elections return.

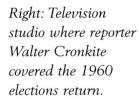

John F. Kennedy Library and Museum

"Libraries are memories," John Kennedy once said, "and in this library you will have the memory of an extraordinary American." Though he was speaking of the Robert Frost Library in Amherst, Massachusetts, his prophetic words also describe the presidential library and museum later built in his honor. Located on Columbia Point near the University of Massachusetts—Boston campus, the John F. Kennedy Library and Museum overlooks Boston Harbor south of the city. The site is a splendid tribute to a navy man who loved the ocean, and architect I.M.Pei's building beautifully captures the setting with a 115-foot high glass pavilion. Outside near the water sits Kennedy's sailboat *Victura*, a silent reminder of the President's favorite pastime. "His passion for the sea would have made him a great explorer," his brother Edward declared.

The Kennedy Library has a long history of community outreach and educational programming that make it more than a simple repository of documents for scholars. Since 1989, for instance, it has hosted the prestigious Profiles in Courage Award ceremony, so named for Kennedy's 1957 Pulitzer prize–winning book about principled politicians. Winners of the non-partisan award, which is personally handed out by Kennedy family members on JFK's birthday, have included Senators John McCain and Russell Feingold, who together sponsored legislation regulating federal campaign contributions. In 2001, the award went to former President Gerald Ford for his controversial pardon of Richard Nixon in 1974, a decision that some believe cost him the presidency two years later. The previous year had seen California state senator Hilda Solis become the first female honoree for her environmental efforts.

The Library is especially active in educating today's youth, who have no recollection of Kennedy or the monumental events that defined his presidency. Yet when the library first opened, adults who remembered him treated it as a shrine to their fallen hero, though the President is not buried on the site.

Larz Anderson Auto Museum

Massachusetts has a history of transportation innovation. While still a part of the British Empire, Boston had a reputation for producing handsome horse-drawn carriages and sturdy sailing vessels. As the cradle of American industry in the nineteenth century, the Bay State constructed the nation's first subway system in Boston and built some of the first American automobiles. The Duryea brothers of Springfield are credited with designing a gasoline-powered vehicle as early as 1897. And while that western Massachusetts city later became famous as the home of Indian motorcycles, it was Sylvester Roper of Boston's Roxbury neighborhood who developed the steam-powered prototype that some consider the first motorcycle. It is thus quite fitting that Massachusetts should have what may well be the oldest private automobile collection in the United States, albeit one composed mostly of foreign-made cars.

The European flair of Brookline's Larz Anderson Auto Museum reflects the tastes of its founders, Larz and Isabel Anderson. Larz was born in Paris, but educated in New England at the prestigious Phillips Exeter Academy and later Harvard. It was as a member of the U.S. diplomatic corps in Rome during the 1890s that he met Isabel Weld Perkins, a young Massachusetts debutante who had inherited millions from her maternal grandfather's shipping empire. They married back in Boston in 1897 and soon afterward bought their first automobile, the rare Winton Runabout. In the days before Henry Ford promised to "democratize the automobile," sales were largely restricted to wealthy families such as the Andersons, who would accumulate over thirty motorcars in their collection. Contrary to popular belief, however, the Andersons did not keep every car they ever owned, only their favorites.

Though they also owned homes in Washington, D.C. and New Hampshire, Larz and Isabel stored their automobiles at their sixty-four acre Brookline estate on property once owned by her grandfather. Larz's death ten years later and his wife's passing in 1948 might have ended the museum had Isabel not made provisions in her will to protect it. The town of Brookline inherited the Anderson estate, while the Veteran Motor Car Club of America operated the museum.

In recent years, the Auto Museum has reinvented itself under innovative new directors, making it well worth the drive to visit. It regularly hosts outdoor festivals and auctions and has even begun a Carriage House Concert Series. Themed exhibitions feature period vehicles loaned from antique collectors and other museums. Past examples include "The Fabulous Fifties," "Muscle Cars: Power to Burn," and "L'automobile," which focused on such French beauties as Peugeots, Renaults, and Delahayes. New England's automotive tradition was celebrated in the popular 1989 exhibition "Putting America on Wheels: New England Paves the Way." To enhance the viewing experience, visitors are now able to walk around and between the cars, watch films on the history of the automobile, and see vintage prints and photos.

Around the Hub

Massachusetts Institute of Technology

"*Mens et Manus*," meaning "Mind and Hand," is the proud motto of the Massachusetts Institute of Technology, better known as M.I.T. It reflects the vision for the school put forward by its founder, William Barton Rogers, who believed in the practical application of higher learning to better society. As the son of an Irish-born chemistry professor, Rogers and his brothers had been exposed to the wonders of science from an early age. After attending the College of William and Mary in the 1820s, he taught for a while in Maryland before returning to William and Mary as a professor. But it was while teaching at the University of Virginia in the 1840s that he began to seriously consider creating a polytechnic school dedicated especially to the sciences, which often received only secondary consideration at liberal arts colleges.

Boston's developing Back Bay neighborhood was where Rogers envisioned establishing the new school. He admired the "Yankee ingenuity" of New England industrialists as well as the region's historic commitment to education embodied in such institutions as Harvard. Further incentives were provided by his marriage to a Boston native and by the Governor's support for educational institutions in the Back Bay. A charter incorporating the Massachusetts Institute of Technology was granted in April of 1861, but the outbreak of the Civil War that same month made fundraising and student recruiting difficult. Temporary quarters were established in downtown Boston while Rogers awaited completion of a more permanent home not far from Copley Square.

With the war over and construction of the new campus complete in 1866, M.I.T. began carving out its reputation for academic excellence. It established the nation's first architectural program, developed a highly-praised civil engineering department, and earned accolades for its innovative approaches to learning. Alexander Graham Bell used its facilities; Thomas Edison's son studied there, as did members of the du Pont family; and in 1873 Ellen Swallow Richards became the school's first female graduate. In fact, M.I.T. became so well respected that wealthy Harvard repeatedly tried to buy the cash-strapped Institute to shore up its own weakness in the sciences. A sale nearly happened in 1904, but M.I.T. faculty and alumni vigorously protested and the purchase became hopelessly entangled in legal difficulties.

Instead of being absorbed by Harvard, M.I.T. became its next-door neighbor in 1916. President Richard C. Maclaurin oversaw the purchase of forty-six acres along the Cambridge side of the Charles River, after rejecting an offer to relocate the school to Springfield, Massachusetts and ignoring warnings from Harvard that the move would imperil both colleges. To

Killian Court and The Great Dome.

Previous page: Charles River.

140

finance construction of a new campus, he turned to wealthy businessmen and philanthropists, such as George Eastman of Eastman Kodak, who shared his vision for the school. Armed with millions, Maclaurins hired alum William Welles Bosworth to design the complex of buildings that would bear the president's name. All this from a man who, by his own admission, had "often criticized the educational authorities for acting as if buildings make the institution."

The most distinctive features of the Maclaurin Buildings are the beautiful courtyard they surround and the Great Dome that forms their focal point. Commencement ceremonies are usually held in the Great Court, also known as Killian Court, with the Great Dome providing a striking backdrop. Below ground lie passageways that connect campus buildings and enable students to avoid harsh New England winters. In typical M.I.T. fashion, most buildings are referred to by number rather than name, a system that often disorients outsiders.

At the opposite end of the architectural spectrum from the Maclaurins Buildings stands the Ray and Maria Stata Center for Computer, Information, and Intelligence Sciences, opened in 2004. The Statas donated $25 million toward the construction of a $285 million building that Cambridge mayor Michael A. Sullivan initially thought "looked like something my kids built and then took a hammer to." More money for the facility, $20 million to be exact, came from Microsoft's Bill Gates, who had once attended rival Harvard. Architect Frank O. Gehry's whimsical Stata Center replaced the simple, yet much-loved Building 20 that had occupied the site since World War II.

Born of military necessity, Building 20 housed part of a radiation laboratory where researchers worked on advancing Allied radar technology. The infusion of federal dollars and military contracts during World War II and the Cold War transformed M.I.T. into the nation's premiere scientific research institution in the 1950s and kept Building 20 bustling for decades. Its demolition in 1998 to make way for the Stata Center reflected the historic changes that had ended the Cold War and signaled the end of an era at M.I.T.

Times may have changed, but M.I.T. remains an elite institution. It has produced fifty-nine Nobel Prize winners from the ranks of its alumni and faculty, nearly half of them in the field of physics. Newspaper and magazine polls consistently rate M.I.T. as one of the most selective and rigorous schools in the country. "The thing that really struck me when I first got to M.I.T.," alumna Eleni Digenis told the *Boston Globe* in 1994, "was that everyone just seemed so totally focused." Perhaps that's why the school chose the industrious beaver as its mascot and even named its sports teams the Engineers.

Harvard University

If Boston is the self-styled "Athens of America," then Harvard University, located across the Charles River in nearby Cambridge, is its Lyceum. Not only is Harvard the oldest institution of higher education in the United States, its name remains synonymous with academic excellence over three centuries after its 1636 founding. It is a school steeped in tradition, from its ancient architecture to its forty Nobel Prize winners. Seven American presidents have graduated from Harvard, as have many of the nation's top lawyers, doctors, and business executives. Though it is often accused of a conservative and elitist character, the university's renowned faculty routinely produces innovative, cutting edge research that transforms our understanding of the world, whether it concerns the discovery of distant galaxies or the latest breakthrough in cancer treatment. Indeed, Harvard has always been a school that forges the future while sustaining the past.

Stepping into Harvard Yard, one immediately senses the history that surrounds the venerable institution. The Puritans founded the school as a place to provide the Massachusetts Bay Colony with its own trained ministry. Toward this end, The Reverend John Harvard willed his extensive personal library and much of his estate to the fledgling college when he died in 1638. Officials were so thankful for his generosity that they named the school in his honor. Tragically, nearly all of the minister's 400 books were lost in a fire that swept through the campus in 1764.

Yet the school has never forgotten Harvard's deed, even if it has sometimes mistaken the particulars. In 1884, it unveiled a bronze statue of the benefactor designed by Daniel Chester French, best known for his work on the Lincoln Memorial in Washington, D.C. The sculpture has since become known as "The Statue of Three Lies" for fabricating an image of Harvard, whose likeness was never set to canvas, and mislabeling

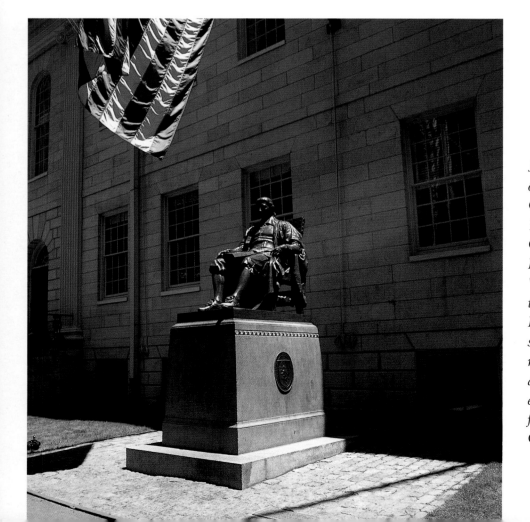

John Harvard statue located in front of University Hall (designed by Charles Bulfinch and completed in 1815), was cast in 1884 by Daniel Chester French (sculptor of the Lincoln Memorial) and is known as "The Statue of Three Lies." Although the inscription reads "John Harvard, Founder, 1638," none of these three statements is true. The seated figure is not really John Harvard, since no authentic pictures of Mr. Harvard existed; John Harvard was not the founder of Harvard College; and the College was founded in 1636.

Harvard Square.

him as the school's 1638 founder. He may not have been the founder, but he is the university's mascot. Students and visitors alike rub the statue's left shoe for good luck.

Harvard's statue is situated in front of University Hall, which Charles Bulfinch designed for his alma mater in 1814. The building was supposed to feature one of the architect's signature cupolas, but the expense proved prohibitive. It did, however, include a chapel used until construction of Appleton Chapel in the 1850s. That building was located behind University Hall to the east, a site now occupied by the familiar white spire of Memorial Chapel. The chapel was dedicated in 1932 to the memory of Harvard

men killed in World War I. Interestingly, it also memorializes four students who served in the German army, an honor not accorded to the school's Confederate soldiers in the 1878 Memorial Hall for the Union dead.

Since its opening, Memorial Chapel has also commemorated students who perished in wars as recent as Vietnam. In November of 2001, the university erected a plaque honoring three graduates of Radcliffe, Harvard's historic sister school for women, who lost their lives in World War I. It was another step in moving the campus toward more complete gender integration and combating lingering allegations of discrimination against women. Unfortunately, those efforts suffered a setback in 2005 when Harvard's president, Lawrence H. Summers, suggested that men and women might have different intellectual capacities for the sciences. He later apologized for the comment after a firestorm of protest, promising to take a more tactful approach in the future.

The president's office is located in Massachusetts Hall, the oldest building on campus. The 1720 brick structure stands opposite University Hall to the west, across the Old Yard. It was originally used as a dormitory, and during the siege of Boston in 1775 and 1776 it acted as a barracks for the Continental troops of George Washington. The General (before he became President) briefly used the wooden Wadsworth House, built in 1726 for the college's president, as his headquarters. Today it serves as the Alumni Office. Nearby Matthews Hall is the approximate location of Harvard's Indian school, which provided religious training for a handful of Christian Indians in the seventeenth century.

Harvard's religious roots remain visible in a number of ways, including the school song "Fair Harvard," which concludes with the lines "Be the herald of light, and the bearer of love/ Till the stock of the Puritans die." The university also boasts one of the nation's best divinity schools, though it is no longer affiliated with one particular faith. The curriculum has also diversified since its colonial days, when students were required to take courses in religion, logic, ethics, Hebrew, and metaphysics among others. Neither has Harvard sustained its traditional ranking system based on family status rather than academic merit. For a time regarded as "a fashionable finishing school for young gentlemen," according to Samuel Eliot Morison, Harvard is now arguably more diverse and dynamic than at any time in its storied history.

Architecture building

Museum of Science

In a city chock full of cultural museums, from those reflecting Boston's storied history to others aimed at the fine arts, the Museum of Science offers a decidedly different experience, yet one as quintessentially Boston as any old Brahmin exposition. Scientific inquiry had been a hallmark of the City upon a Hill at least as far back as Reverend Cotton Mather's membership in the Royal Society of London. Science courses were part of the Harvard curriculum in the colonial era, and the college established a medical school even before the American Revolution had ended. Several local

"Where's what around Boston" exhibit.

doctors evinced an interest in the sciences and natural history, prompting them to form the Boston Society of Natural History in 1830. From this group of amateur naturalists sprang the New England Museum of Natural History that served as the nineteenth-century predecessor to the Museum of Science. For decades after the Civil War, the museum shared a block in the Back Bay with the Massachusetts Institute of Technology, whose first president, William Barton Rogers, was also a member of the Boston Society of Natural History.

The modern Museum of Science was a creation of the same post-World War II emphasis on science that pushed M.I.T. to the forefront of scientific research. Responding to this new cultural climate, the museum's director Bradford Washburn, a world-famous mountain climber,

dropped the traditional "natural history" designation from its title in favor of a new identity as a science museum. He also relocated the museum to its current position overlooking the Charles River in downtown Boston, making the Museum of Science one of the early examples of post-war urban redevelopment.

Today the Museum of Science attracts over 1.5 million visitors annually, a figure that many other local museums can only dream about. Museum officials work especially hard to instill an appreciation for science in children, as evidenced by the hundreds of school groups that visit every year. Teaching aids and science workshops are also made available to area educators. And in 2005, the museum announced that it would offer free admission to children in the Boston public school system to encourage their interest in science.

Weeks Memorial Footbridge

The Weeks Memorial Footbridge may not be the largest or longest bridge to span the Charles River, but it is certainly the most charming. Built in the 1920s, the bridge honors the broker and politician John Wingate Weeks, who served as Secretary of War under the Republican administrations of Warren Harding and Calvin Coolidge.

The site chosen for the bridge would connect the new Harvard School of Business with the rest of the campus on the Cambridge side of the river. The renowned architectural firm of McKim, Mead, and White, most famous for remodeling the White House, designed the brick and limestone bridge to harmonize with the buildings they had created for the Business School. The Weeks Memorial Footbridge was dedicated in 1927.

Since its opening, the footbridge has become a site of celebration as well as a utilitarian means of conveyance. It especially appeals to those with a passion for romance and nature. The Tango Society of Boston used the Weeks Bridge as the setting for its "Tango by Moonlight" affair in 2000, and the Charles River Conservancy that helps manage the bridge holds its "RiverSing" festival there to mark the autumnal equinox. Thanks to the fundraising efforts of the Conservancy, Harvard University, and the LEF Foundation, the Weeks Memorial Footbridge was outfitted with permanent light fixtures in 2004, making it a bit less romantic, perhaps, but more accessible.

Minute Man National Historical Park

Above: Ralph Waldo Emerson coined the phrase "the shot heard 'round the world" to describe the significance of the brief battle which took place at the North Bridge.

Since the famous "Shot Heard 'Round the World" in April of 1775, the history of Boston has been inextricably linked with that of two small villages in the Massachusetts countryside, Lexington and Concord. The British occupation of Boston in 1774 had scattered its population and forced Revolutionary leaders to find safe refuge in the colony's interior. Their presence helped rouse formerly apathetic farming communities that typically cared more about planting than politics. Concord, some twenty miles from Boston, soon became a major center of resistance, hosting the patriots' Provincial Congress and stockpiling munitions for a possible war.

In the meantime, royal officials were pressuring General Thomas Gage, commander of British troops in Boston, to move decisively to break up the rebellion. He had already ordered raids against suspected stores of arms in

Somerville and Salem, but more force was deemed necessary to scare the New Englanders into submission. Plans were accordingly made to seize the arms at Concord and perhaps capture two patriot leaders believed to be in the area, John Hancock and Samuel Adams. But before the expeditionary force could assemble along the edge of Boston Common, Paul Revere and other messengers had begun warning the countryside that the Regulars, as British soldiers were commonly called, were appearing.

Among the towns Revere alarmed before capture by a British patrol was Lexington, which lay directly in the path of the British advance toward Concord. In the early hours of April 19, 1775, Lexington's militia mustered

Below: The Minute Man statue was sculpted by Daniel Chester to honor the citizen-soldier of 1775.

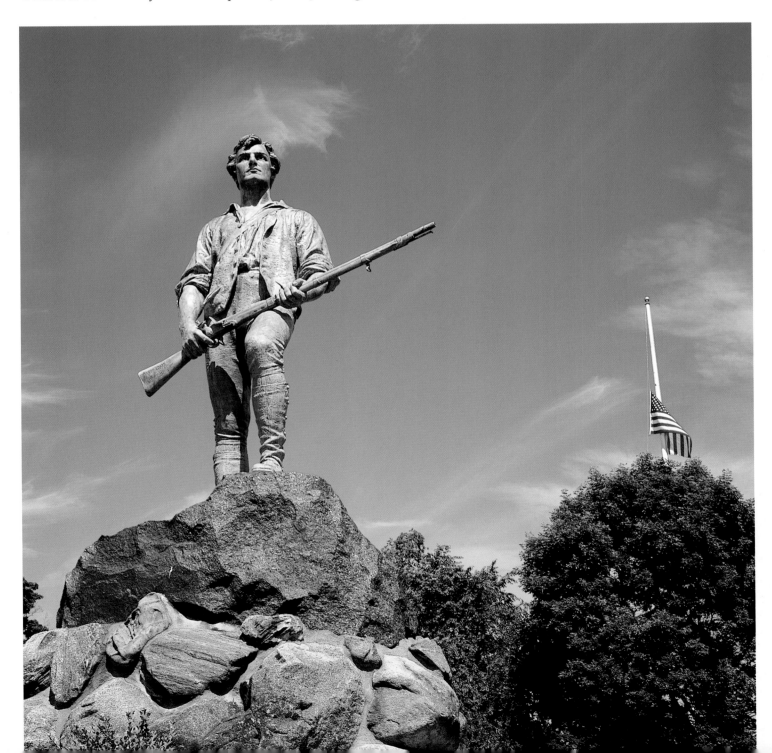

on the Common under the command of Captain John Parker, a forty-six-year-old farmer and veteran of the French and Indian War. Despite suffering from tuberculosis, Parker stood in the cool, windy weather with his men, waiting for the enemy to arrive. Conflicting reports about British movements prompted some to retire to nearby Buckman's Tavern, however, until the sounds of approaching soldiers sent them scurrying back onto the Common around 4:30 a.m.

Outnumbered nearly four to one, Parker told his men to stand firm but not to fire as the Redcoats filed in around them. "[I]f they want to have a

Below: Hartwell Tavern—a 1733 building with later additions— was not only a typical country inn of the period, but it was also the scene of fighting along Battle Road.

war let it begin here," he reportedly said. The words proved prophetic, for while British officers negotiated with Parker to end the standoff, a shot rang out. To this day, it is unclear who fired first, but in the confusion that followed seven militiamen were killed and nine others wounded. The Revolutionary War had begun.

Parker would gain his revenge later that day as the wearied British soldiers returned from Concord and marched right into an ambush by Lexington militia. To honor Parker's heroic stand for American freedom, the town erected Henry H. Kitson's bronze statue of him in 1900. It stands defiantly atop an outcropping of boulders presumably taken from a stone wall used on the day of the battle. Facing east toward Boston, with the American flag at its back, the statue also marks the direction of the approaching British column. In 1965, the federal government made the flag on Lexington's

John Meriam's House, at Meriam's Corner, is one of the oldest houses in Concord, MA. The shots exchanged here between colonial militia and British troops began the fighting along the Battle Road that continued for 16 miles.

Meriam's Corner

Battle Green one of only a handful nationwide that is to be flown continuously. The state of Massachusetts commemorates the historic events at Lexington and Concord annually with Patriot's Day. The highlight of this April 19th holiday is a re-enactment of Parker's clash with the British along with events such as the Boston Marathon and a Red Sox baseball game at Fenway Park.

Once the home of Samuel Whitney, muster master for the Concord Minute Men, The Wayside gained fame in the 19th century through three literary families. Louisa May Alcott's childhood here inspired her scenes in Little Women. Nathaniel Hawthorne named it The Wayside; Margaret Sidney, author of Five Little Peppers, preserved this "Home of Authors."

Salem Witch Trials Tercentenary Memorial

Though its name means "peace" in Hebrew, Salem has come to symbolize intolerance in the American cultural lexicon. What began as a strange affliction among a group of young girls ended with the execution of twenty people for the crime of witchcraft in the summer of 1692. Already convinced that Satan was tormenting their fair town, officials ignored denials of guilt and pleas for mercy from the accused.

Theories abound as to why witchcraft hysteria gripped Salem. Might resentful farm families have lodged false accusations against those associated with the seaport's more prosperous commercial order? New England in the 1690s was also caught in the coils of a war that many Puritans saw as divine punishment for their sinful ways. Perhaps the anxiety and sense of impending doom caused a reactionary search for scapegoats within the community.

The Salem Witch Trials Tercentenary Memorial offers a more dignified and solemn reminder of the awful consequences created by intolerance. Designed by architect Jim Cutler and artist Maggie Smith, the memorial was dedicated in 1992 as part of Salem's tercentenary commemoration of the witch trials. Its themes, according to Cutler, are deafness, silence, and memory, which are represented in several ways. The accused are allowed to speak for themselves through quotes etched in stone, yet the walls cut off their words before being completed, a symbol of society's indifference to their pleas.

"If it was the last moment I was to live, God knows I am innocent..."
—Elizabeth Howe, hanged July 19, 1692

Salem Maritime National Historic Site

Established in 1938, the Salem Maritime National Historic Site was the first of its kind in the United States, and federal officials could hardly have picked a better place to launch their preservation program. Salem began as a small fishing port in 1626, predating Boston by a few years. In fact, the Winthrop fleet that would later found Boston arrived first in Salem in 1630 before heading south. Though it could not match Boston in wealth, size and power, Salem did become an important shipping center for fish and timber in the colonial period, one of several North Shore seaports that gave Boston merchants a run for their money. The British blockade and occupation of Boston in 1774 steered business toward Salem, which also became the leading center of privateering activity during the Revolutionary War.

Thanks in part to the success of its wartime privateers, who are believed to have raided over four hundred British ships, the seaport emerged from the Revolution primed to enter new markets and was an early player in the lucrative China trade. This era of commercial expansion is commemorated with the *Friendship*, a full-scale reproduction of the 1797 ship that made some fifteen international voyages before being captured by the British during the War of 1812. Researchers were able to estimate its dimensions and design using period paintings as well as the ship's logs. The original 342-ton *Friendship* would have brought spices, teas, and other foreign goods from Far Eastern ports to eager New England customers. Salem's renowned Peabody-Essex Museum, founded in 1799, contains many Chinese export items acquired by Salem merchants in these flush years. There one can also find an 1805 oil painting of the *Friendship* returning home to Salem along with a model of the original used to create the replica.

Opposite: Friendship, a reconstruction of a 171-foot three-masted Salem East Indiaman built in 1797, arrived on September 1, 1998 at the National Park Service's Salem Maritime National Historic Site in Salem, after two years of construction at Scarano Boat Building in Albany. She is the largest wooden, Coast Guard certified, sailing vessel to be built in New England in more than a century.

Top left: The lighthouse on Derby Wharf, with others at Pickering Point on Winter Island and Hospital Point in Beverly, was built in 1871 to "complete the system for the Harbor of Salem."

Top right: The Custom House (1819) represented the U.S. Government in the port. Permits to land cargo, seamen's protection certificates, and ships measurements certificates were issued here.

Index